Psychological Foundation of Education

Srinibas Bhattacharya

ATLANTIC

PUBLISHERS & DISTRIBUTORS (P) LTD

Published by

ATLANTIC

PUBLISHERS & DISTRIBUTORS (P) LTD

7/22, Ansari Road, Darya Ganj, New Delhi-110002
Phones : +91-11-40775252, 40775214, 23273880, 23275880
Fax : +91-11-23285873
Web : www.atlanticbooks.com
E-mail : orders@atlanticbooks.com

Branch Office: Chennai
Phones : +91-44-48531784, 28291383
E-mail : chennai@atlanticbooks.com

Printed & bound in India by Atlantic Print Services

PREFACE

Psychology has a very significant bearing on education because of its influence on the various factors related to learning and teaching. The fundamental principles in psychology has tremendous impact on education and teaching.

Without the knowledge of psychology a teacher is at a loss to understand to needs and problems in a child's life.

Psychology provides the key to know the individual differences and meets them with appropriate educational programmes. It also helps the teachers to offer guidance and counselling to the pupils.

In fact, psychology places education on a scientific basis and brings dignity to education as a discipline.

The experimental approach has become feasible because of the contribution of psychology to education.

Powers and propensities of mind have been analysed with the help of psychological techniques and measurement of mind has been a reality with the introduction of psychology as an objective science. Besides it has been possible to mark out the different areas of mental operation. The mental process and the product, its structure and function have been discussed at length in this section for bringing out the practical value of psychological approach.

SRINIBAS BHATTACHARYA

CONTENTS

PART III
PSYCHOLOGICAL FOUNDATION OF EDUCATION

1
INTRODUCTION

The Psychological Foundation of Education is obviously a very significant section for studying the interaction between psychology and education. Child psychology deals with the mental structure and function of a child. Psychology provides the bricks and mortar for laying the foundation of education on a scientific basis. It has much to offer for raising the status of education as a social science.

As described in the following pages, Psychology deals with instincts and emotions, abilities and interest, individual differences and personality. There bearing on education is of vital importance to the parents, teachers and social workers.

One has to see what psychology contributes to education and education offers to psychology. The bearning of one on the other has to be considered for making the study of this foundation meaningful.

The present decade has focussed on experimentation in the field of learning and teaching in the perspective of behavioural sciences.

PSYCHOLOGY AND EDUCATION : AN INTRODUCTION

Psychology is a growing subject. It is a developing science extending its branches in different spheres.

One of the important functions of psychology today is to offer guidance of various types on the basis of individual differences. There are many approaches to the study of an individual and very recently emphasis has been shifted from ability testing to the study of personality as a whole. As a result, various techniques of personality measurement have been evolved.

It is obvious that any research in psychology today demands an objective analysis of data. With a view to arriving at certain dependable conclusions, statistics has become an indispensable tool.

In spite of the suggested techniques for analysis of data various problems often arise in the field of investigation.

The modern tendency is, therefore, to develop such statistical tools as to eliminate the element of subjective judgement entering so much into its operation. Wringley (1956) has focussed attention upon these limitations of factor analysis and has discussed the prospect of a further analysis named as quartimax analysis.

Another chapter has been opened by psychologists of the day and that is on social psychology. The importance of this branch of psychology is being increasingly felt.

The methods of modern psychology are essentially those of natural science. It is improper perhaps to advocate a divorce between psychology and natural science on the ground of differences in method. The question, therefore, arises, "Is there any method of formulating mind and consciousness so that their study may be brought more fully within the orbit of the natural sciences ?"

Challenge to experimental psychology has to be accepted and a middle course found. A psychologist should accept in principle the practical demands which the community makes upon him. But there is no assurance that every challenge will lead to a quick solution. Truth is not always found by those who seek it. Some time it emerges almost by accident. The new and vital challenges of study may bring with them a new spirit of urgency and reality. Every challenge comes with a risk, no doubt.

MODERN TRENDS IN PSYCHOLOGY AND EDUCATION

Psychology today has its challenges from the contemporary world of social sciences. The primary aim of psychological science is to understand human nature. The secondary aim is to serve society. It is probable that the psychologist, who works in the social field will be confronted with a number of challenges. Obviously psychology at present is yet incapable of solving a few human and social problems.

We see an increasing concern with the problems of mind and consciousness today. A marked development of research in the area of social psychology is observed in view of the new challenges. As a science of behaviour and experience psychology has a wider scope of application than before. The study of human behaviour in groups is a recent development and is, confronted with a number of problems.

There are certain typical issues involved in psychological study. In most cases psychology as a growing science has to depend mainly on observations. This is unsatisfactory because of the subjective nature of observation as a technique. Nevertheless, this technique cannot be done away with unless a relatively objective method is evolved. Psychology today has extended its scope and assumed a responsible task of discovering new laws and principles. It has also been extended to the classroom situation, in the field of industry and medicine.

EDUCATIONAL PSYCHOLOGY AS A SCIENCE

Educational psychology may be thought of a science with two main points of references human behaviour and education. It is concerned with behavioural questions that are related to the objectives and practices of education. The domain of psychology is rather broad, ranging from the study of the collective behaviour of human beings, to individual differences.

The methods of science are often employed in a systematic fashion and some techniques for applying the knowledge to practical ends in educational settings are used by educational psychology.

The following questions should be answered by an educational psychologist today :

1. How are children's abilities, knowledge and effective characteristics related to objectives of education ?
2. How does knowledge of learning process and theories contribute to more efficient learning and teaching ?
3. How do characteristics of the learner effect his readiness to learn and efficiency of learning ?
4. How do characteristics of the teacher affect pupil learning?
5. How do the behaviours of the teacher and the student affect efficiency of learning ?

New horizons in educational psychology are, thus inviting the attention of the educationists and psychologists.

The contribution of educational psychology may be broken down into two related categories :

(a) Educational psychology as a body of information and an avenue of research activity can help in the generation of educational hypothesis.

(b) It also helps to formulate hypotheses for particular purposes.

Educational psychology contributes a lot to the area of teacning and learning as well as a behavioural science applied in the class-room situation. Its main contribution lies in the understanding of the pupils as well as developing systematic programmes, according to the potentials and needs of the pupils and the community. As a growing science it has a lot more to offer in building hypothesis around the interaction between human factors involved in education. As a source of information it helps the teacher to come to right decision on the basis of what he knows about individual difference. Educational psychology has a definite role in providing insight into the processes of learning and teaching as well as the knowledge of group dynamics for underlying each learning situation. In essence, psychology as a science promotes action researches among teachers in classroom situation by way of helping them to form intelligent Hypothesis.

Thus Educational psychology is the application of psychological findings in the field of Education. It is obviously an applied discipline trying to combine the two different areas viz., psychology and Education. In a school situation the teacher has not only to know the subject, he has to know the pupils and their personality and problems as well. Besides, he has to know the developmental characteristics of the learner in addition to his individual differences. Moreover, as a teacher he needs to develop appropriate methods of teaching for meeting the individual differences. Psychology of Education helps the teacher to probe into and develop skills for effective functioning. In addition to the tasks mentioned before, the teacher has to function as an evaluator for measuring the outcome of his teaching. Thus, the various roles and functions of a teacher are facilitated by his knowledge and application of Educational psychology. In short, educational psychology provides a frame-work for looking at the learner, the learning process and the learning situation together. Teaching is thus based upon mastery of three areas :-

(a) Knowledge and concept,

(b) Teaching skills, and

(c) Decision-making skills.

The knowledge of Educational psychology helps a teacher to be more aware of class room behaviour, to interpret the significance of such behaviour and to plan purposeful strategy for bringing the desired changes in the pupils' behaviour. In other words. a major role of

Educational psychology is to make assumptions about the conditions that facilitate learning and to collect data for testing the hypothesis.

As mentioned earlier, a teacher has not only to teach, he has to make decision. Successful teachers hold realistic attitude towards students. They have to inspire and make decision in formulating effective methods for reaching the strategies. Psychology of Education orients a teacher to form the strategies as well as provides the skill to reach them.

To day we find most of the class rooms crowded and disorganised. He is perplexed with a number of challenges. It is not easy for him to solve the problems beyond his control. In most cases the syllabus is unwieldy and the students are not motivated. Moreover, there is a lot of unrest among the younger generation leading to anti-social activities. The knowledge of psychology of Education helps a teacher to meet some to these challenges.

NEW HORIZON IN EDUCATIONAL PSYCHOLOGY

The psychological foundation of education can hardly be ignored because of its relevance to teaching, learning as well as teacher's functioning. Recently the psychological approach to the class-room problems has been considered superior to other approaches. Particularly the behaviouristic model has been recognised and recommended today. The need for considering teaching as a behaviour involving communication and skill is acknowledged. Thus psychology of education is expected to provide insight into the area of pupil's behaviour and learning process. Books on educational psychology are opening new frontiers for dealing with intricate problems of motivation and group interactions. Today experiments are being conducted in the area of group dynamics for explaining certain complex behaviour patterns leading to indiscipline and unrest among students. Moreover, the social and emotional problems in the class-room are receiving attention of the psychologists. In fact, new areas of education and psychology are showing up with their varied dimensions. The teacher is not only a giver of information, he is an explorer and experimentor applying his knowledge of psychology in practical field of learning and teaching.

New experimentations are being carried on educational technology as well. This includes technology of teaching as well as programmed instruction. By educational technology the behaviourists put forward the following concept. It is a systematic application of scientific knowledge about teaching, learning and conditions of learning to improve the efficiency of teaching and training. Thus teaching has been considered as a science and attempt has been made to analyse the process of teaching with reference to various components. Various strategies have been developed for improving the approach to stimulate a learner at the memory, understanding and reflecting levels.

Another extension of the horizon of educational psychology is programmed instruction. Although skinner's operant conditioning is the basis of this new approach, various experimentations have been made for developing remedial programmes in the areas of learning.

It is interesting to note that a confusion still exists around what should be the scope of educational psychology. The traditional approach was to deal with the psychology of individual differences and theories of learning separately without discussing the educational implications and their relevance to or application in the educational setting. Only recently attempts are being made for an integrated approach so that the methods and principles of psychology are projected in the actual class-room situation. Emphasis is being laid on the role of teachers and analysis of teaching for making a realistic approach to education. Various new dimensions have been added to dynamics of student behaviour for facilitating the understanding of the needs and problems.

In the area of educational psychology an integrated approach is being attempted by synthesizing the teaching learning process in the perspective of teacher's function. This approach has gone a long way in making educational psychology more meaningful and relevant to a practising teacher. Behaviouristic and applied psychology is gaining more grounds, while simple pedagogy with its theories is losing ground.

2

SOME BASIC FACTORS

SENSATION AND PERCEPTION

Senses are the gateways to learning. We get our experience through sensation. Our sense organs are the windows of the soul. We derive our knowledge of the reality with the help of the five sense organs which respond typically to different stimuli. We become conscious of the various aspects of reality through our sensation. A sensation is a response when some sense organ is stimulated. Every sense organ has the capacity to be stimulated in response to a kind of stimulus. Our eyes respond at the sight of an object while our ears help us to hear a sound (stimulus)

There are branches or endings of sensory neurons within each sense organ which help to arouse the excitement and pass it on to the central nervous system. A sensation is a response or reaction aroused in us by the stimulus. This is an act of the sense organ which sends nerve currents to the sensory centres of the brain. It is the first response of the brain but the activity of the nerve cells at the sense organ does not by itself constitute the sensation. It involves an elementary mental process as well.

Each sense organ has its own set of neurons which are connected with a particular part of the brain or spinal chord. The type of stimulus to which every sense organ is adapted to respond is called the appropriate stimulus.

It is apparent that external objects impinge upon our sense organs and arouse sensation. We only receive the impressions without acting. Thus a sensation depends upon the brain response, the activity of sensory cells and nerves but less on the stimulus.

Many of our organic sensations are stimulated from within while a number of stimuli is external. For example hunger and thirst are our organic sensations stimulated from within.

Perception is sensation plus meaning. It involves sensation and an interpretation of the sensation. We sense qualities like colours sound, taste, smell etc. while perception interprets them as objects. The two processes involved in perception standout in our day to day experience.

The congnitive functioning of the mind makes perception complete. Our thought and interpretation, our experience and analysis contribute to the perceptual process.

Sensation and perception are both important for the purpose of education. The child gains experience and knowledge through the sense organs, no doubt, but his real knowledge of the reality and its perspectives is the outcome of perception. In short, sense perception makes a person conscious of the object and its meaning. The fusion of various sense qualities which are presented together in consciousness constitute the elements of meaning. Thus perception motivates more than a combination of sensations. According to the Gestalt view the total structure patterns of configuration come into play for forming perception. An experience of the totality or unalyzable whole is the keynote to perception. Mind works as a whole and responds to the whole situation. The awareness of the relation steps between the parts comprising the whole and brings the total perception. Each of our perceptions is a unique configuration pattern of relationships.

Perceptional Development in Children

Perception varies as the product of varied experiences. Children differ in forming impressions around the same stimulus because of different interpretation. The children's perceptions obviously differ from those of adults.

The child has experience and his sense organs can hardly perceive qualities and things of relationship. Childhood is described as a period of confusion. Every stimulus including colour, sound and shape remains vague and indefinite. The differentiation is slow and gradual. Children's perception are less analytical as they lack attention to details. Secondly the child needs to have a stronger stimulus to form a perception than an adult. Only bright things or sounds are perceived by him if repeated.

Perception is thus a process of "taking in". It is a mental assimilation of a new presentation. The stock of ideas and the stored experience form the perceptive mass which differs with different individuals. Sense training has been emphasized by Montessori as an effective method of child development. Sensory experience contributes to perceptual development which aims to cultivate observation. Observation implies thinking and ideas and depends on imagination, reasoning or sense perception.

Perception and Personality

Personality depends mainly on how one perceives himself and his environment. Self knowledge has been rightly emphasized in the upanishads as much depends upon ones relationship with the world around him. The relationship is congenial and conducive if ones perception about himself is happy and healthy.

Education helps to form perception in oneself in relation to reality. If the reality orientation is positive and strong there is every chance of happiness.

A healthy attitude is the outcome of positive perception of reality and relationship.

A balanced healthy educational programme is needed most in education to day.

INSTINCTS AND EMOTIONS

Instinct is a native behaviour. It is an innate disposition, a tendency to respond in a particular way to specific stimuli. McDongall defined instinct as an innate disposition which determines an organism to perceive or pay attention to any object of a certain class and to experience in its presence a certain emotional excitement which finds expression in a specific mode of behaviour in relation to that object.

There are certain characteristics of Instincts as follows :

(1) Instinctive behaviour is innate or native and not acquired or learnt.

(2) It is more a tendency to act or behave in a particular way.

(3) Instincts are universal.

(4) They do not imply any foresight of a useful end although they tend toward the well being of species.

(5) Instinctive responses are capable of modification, adaptation and development.

(6) Lastly, Instinct has its period of appearance, maturity and weakening.

Mr. Dongall believes that every instinct is connected with a specific emotion. He offers the following list :

Instinct	Emotion	Instinct	Emotion
Escape	Fear	Food seeking	Craving for food
Combat	Anger	Appeal	Distress
Repulsion	Disgust	Laughter	Amusement
Curiosity	Wonder		
Parental Instinct	Tender Emotion		
Construction	Feeling of creativeness.		
Acquisition	Feeling of ownership		
Gregariousness	Feeling of togetherness		
Reproduction	Lust		
Self assertain	Elation		
Self Abasenment	Subjection		

While the individual grows he shows various tendencies to satisfy his basic needs.

The children break and build, fear and escape, collect and construct, assert or gets depressed.

The instincts are called specific tendencies which are aroused in definite concrete situations. Besides, there are some specific innate tendencies like play, imitation, suggestion and sympathy. Tensley classifies instincts into three heads, the individual instincts, the social instincts and the sex instinct.

According to Mc Dongall instinct has cognifive affective and conative element. In an instinctive behaviours an individual knows, feels and acts with regard to a particular situation. While Jung suggested three primary instincts of nutrition, sex and heard, Thorndike defined instinct as unlearnt behaviour and left out its emotional aspect.

On a critical analysis one can find a close relation between needs, drive and motives. There are needs for food, protection and physical satisfaction. There are other needs which are less obvious but not less important.

The term 'drive' is also used in the same sense for energy or action which can be modified or affected by different factors or situations.

Instincts their Modification or Sublimation

Instincts can be modified adapted and developed in a variety of ways. Sublimation is the process involving the transformation of the basic instincts into socially approved channels.

For example, the instinct of combat or fighting may be redirected against poverty and ignorance. Similarly the instinct of curiosity may be used for motivating people toward research and experimentation. Similarly the sex instinct may be employed for creative and artistic purposes including poetry, sculpture etc.

All human behaviour arises from some urge or drive. Some of the drives are primitive but they may be modified. Besides, drives, there are social urges and motives. These motives are affected by factors like rewards and punishments.

In view of the complexity of the operation of human drives or motives behind behaviour, a controversy persists around the Theory of Instinct.

The present outlook is shifting from Instinct to needs and propensities. Yet one can not ignore the influence of some innate dispositions or human functioning.

Role of Education of Modifying Instinctive Behaviour

Man is known for his capacity to meet the challenge of the irrational tendencies in him. He has been able to get over some of his primitive tendencies for better adjustment of life and society. His education and experience, his will and determination help him to make the best of the Instincts or emotions he had been endowed with.

Cognition helps man to analyse his strength and weakness for practical purpose. The cognitive domain has thus gained prominence in human behaviour although the role of affective domain is hard to ignore.

Behind every behaviour thinking and feeling work together to determine the mode of operation. As man attains maturity he gains insight into his own nature and control over his impulses. Education helps man to refine his behaviour by modifying instincts.

It is strange that the modern age is encouraging primitive and Instinctive behaviour in spite of the technological advance. Man is learning to conquer nature. He has been making miraculous advance in medical science and space technology but yielding to the basic and primitive instincts of combat and sexuality.

The instincts of the children are not difficult to observe in their everyday life. They show their unending curiosity to know every thing in detail and test the patience of the parents and teachers. It is the duty of the teacher and parents to satisfy their curiosity as far as possible and encourage them to know more about things he comes across.

Similarly the instinct of collection is very dominant among most of the children who show their tendency to hoard things like pebbles, shells, seeds, or even tirifling objects. Trivial things have so dominant an appeal among some children that they irritate the adults by dumping rooms with things of no values to adults. The parents and teachers should respect the children's interest and instinct and treat them sympathetically. They should not offend the children by throwing them away or devaluate the objects they collect with care.

Another dominant instinct among children is the tendency to play. It goes without saying that childhood is the play age. The parents should on no account deprive them of this valuable opportunity to gain satisfaction through play and initiations. The children learn through their parents or adults they observe.

The school and its role in handling the instincts of the children helps children to grow. There must be enough scope for joy and freedom, creative activities and socialisation through schooling.

A rich variety of activity programmes should be introduced in day to day timetable of a Centre for child development. Children should learn through experience, exploration and experiment with joy and freedom.

Teachers should act as friends, philosophers and guides to every child. They should share their experience and joy with the children.

In conclusion, we may say the interest and emotions are the basic elements of personality. As teachers, parents and well wishers we have to be sensitive to the needs, instincts and problems of the children, Sublimation is the most satisfactory way of dealing with instinctive urges. It neither represses them nor gives them a free scope of expression. It is an effective and reconstructive method of utilizing the modes of behaviour. A good and progressive school organizes a variety of co-curricular activities and creates opportunities for recreation through games, dramatics, music and other healthy outlets.

An effective administrator should provide, leadership and guidance to his staff members in helping the children to grow spontaneously.

HABITS AND HABIT-FORMATION

We form habits for reducing stress and strain through practice. Any action which needs much effort and attention at the initial stage gradually becomes easier and less time consuming.

They become automatic and spontaneous through repetition.

Some of the characteristics of habits may be enumerated as follows :

(a) Habit is acquired through repetition in thinking and acting in the same way a number of times which makes the thought and action a part of the habit.

(b) Habit when acquired, does not require any effort and attention.

(c) It becomes automatic and almost mechanical.

(d) Habit facilitates any kind of action through frequent exercise.

Any habit once formed takes time to change. For example anyone who is used to eat rice and curry with finger and hand takes time to change.

Any men used to eating with hand and finger takes sometime to use knife and fork for eating. The modification of the habit takes place gradually as a result of repetition and frequent practices.

They Psychologists offer a different explanation of habit. They assume the role of nervous system when the current flows from one nerve centre to another. They refar to channel or path created or prepared between the two points as a result of the stimulation.

The habitual response, is made as regularly as the reflection or the instinctive tendency. Habitual and instinctive actions are psychical and conscious. They are mental 'phenomena.

One of the advantages of the formation of habits is the economy of physical energy. The performance of habitual action costs little or no effort. In short :

(a) Habit reduces fatigue. For example on the first day of typing one needs more effort than on subsequent days.

(b) Habit makes movements simpler

(c) Habits make our movements more accurate

(d) Habits ensure greater speed

In spite of the advantages of habit formation, habit is not without its limitations. It is mechanical stereotyped and is not adaptable to new situations. It is the mechanising tendency of habit which is hardly appreciated by many. As habit is considered to be opposed to intelligent behaviour, no fixed habit should be formed. It has been rightly said that the best habit is to have no habit.

It is difficult to escape the bondage of habits. Habits kill feeling, and make us insensitive to what may concern us most.

The Role of Habit in Life

Habit have definite role in life as they contribute to health, happiness and efficiency in course of experience. A man develops industriousness through habit, he may also become lazy as a result of his aversion to work. Similarly this honesty and sincerity, shyness or open mindidness depends upon his habit. Even the attitude and outlook depend upon how he spends his early days. Whatever we do, or think tends to become habitual.

In fact, every individual is a bundle of habits. Many believe that childhood is a formative period when good habits are to be formed.

Regularity, punctuality, industriousness, honesty are some of the good habits to be inculcated in early and late childhood.

Similarly social habits, good taste and positive attitudes to life may be developed during later years.

It has been seen that a nation prospers because of good work habits of the people or a community suffers because of bad habits, laziness, addiction and lack of cleanliness. Food habits also influence health and life style. The primitive life styles are examples which show lack of progress and prosperity of the community.

In short, the influence of habit can not be ignored and it is difficult to live without habit. Some how we tend to form habit as a result of practice and continuity of our routine activities.

Every home and school should, therefore, try to inculcate certain fundamental healthy habits during the formative period.

3
INDIVIDUAL DIFFERENCES

In spite of the controversies about learning and other aspects of behaviour, a number of important psychological principles may be widely used by a teacher with confidence. They are, on (a) nature-nurture, (b) learning process, (c) maturation and learning and (d) Individual differences and their implications. The personality of each individual is unique and knowledge of the differences in intelligence, skills, interest, attitude and personality is indeed helpful to a teacher.

The concept of differentiation has been widely used in psychology and the degree of differentiation appears to be an important characteristic of the structure of human abilities. Individual differences have been recognized in early days mainly because of the need for selection and guidance. Thus problem of differentiation remains still unexplored in spite of various attempts to analyse the structure of human abilities and personality. It is rather difficult to analyse the structure of human abilities. It is difficult to say whether the differences in the individual in respect of a particular behaviour or functioning, can be attributed to heredity or environment. As such Individuals vary in personality which is unique. Thus, the differences may be accounted for with reference to personality variables. There are cognitive and affective domains which determine one's perception and feeling and these differences are observed almost in every sphere of functioning. Apart from abilities or capacities, people vary to a bewildering extent in respect of their perception and judgment, attitudes and temperament. Emphasis has so far been laid on the differences in abilities and skills. It is of course, very difficult to represent a person by means of a single index, because all the integrated aspects of an individual's personality are the outcome of a complex process of interaction between the inner propensities and external forces. Scientific doctrines of human abilities and differences are also not in agreement with the popular opinion, that all persons fall into distinct types:

Biological Basis of Personality differences

Individuals develop the peculiarities that they show. The so-called laws of heredity, the extraordinary resemblances and difference between parents and offsprings, all these depend largely on the arrangement and behaviour of the genes, the knowledge of this biological factor is essential to an understanding of the physical aspects of personality. In the light of the present knowledge, it is difficult to predict the inheritance of men, including his physical characteristics. Yet some individuals speak of the transmission of such complicated and culturally influenced factors as mental ability, temperament and attitudes. No one has yet demonstrated the presence of 'genes', controlling intellectual ability or personality characteristics.

The mechanics of inheritance although mapped out are still regarded as too complex to be analysed in full. The general principle of inheritance is that, children resemble their parents and that like begets like. The individual differences of the children even in the same family can be explained to some extent by the principle of variation. As a matter of fact, the germ cells contain different genes which combine in different ways and the permutations and combinations can be varied to bring out the individual differences. Heredity as a source of a variation, may be a very important factor, but this is not all. Numberous studies into the pedigrees of eminent people have clearly indicated that eminence and mental deficiency tend to go hand in hand in families. But this is no clear guidance of the exclusive influences of heredity on individual differences. Systematic studies of correlation between blood-relationship and abilities bring out results which vary from investigation to investigation. It has been found out that in the case of identical twins the correlations come to .8 to .9. In the case of fraternal twins they come to .65 to .70. It is also interesting to note that the correlation between parents and children comes to .40 to .45 and that between grandparents and grand-children comes to .10 to .20. The above result be speaks the scope for variation between individuals even related through common ancestry. Besides, the variation within the people of same heredity, there is another source of variation which is known as environment.

Individual Difference—Their Implication

The hereditarians maintain that education can hardly increase capacity and they also point out that natural difference would find expression regardless of the amount of formal education. The environmentalist, on the other hand, reiterate that the greatest part of individual differences is attributable to discrepancies in cultural and educational opportunities. The present view-point is that of interaction which simply means that both nature and nurture interact in any individual's development. Heredity does not operate in a vacuum. This principle of interaction indicates that nature sets the limits of individual development in regard to various psychological functions but nurture is no less important in determining the extent to which the potentialities shall be developed and the direction in which they should be utilized. Several studies have been conducted on the impact of environment on individual differences. The following concluding observations have been submitted. In the case of fraternal twins, the median coefficient is approximately .70 indicating the influence of both heredity and environment, while in the case of indentical twins, the correlation is .85, showing the importance of heredity alone. Thus, the same kind of nature-nurture inter-relationships have been found in most of the investigations.

There are other sources of variation like race and nationality, sex and age. It is a fact that there are certain racial characteristics which cxplain to a limited extent the relationship between race and individual differences. Studies have been conducted on the relative positions of the various culture groups on intelligence scale and it has been seen that the difference is not too significant to be attributable to the race or nationality alone. There is hardly any evidence of any national superiority in mental abilities, although the differences can be better explained in terms of environment and environmental variation. In fact, the individual differences are so wide even in the same context that the difference due to race or nationality is nothing much significant.

As regards the other factors supposed to contribute to individual differences, sex, age and health deserve special mention. Studies have been carried out and very little evidence has been obtained in favour of the hypothesis of the woman's inferiority in general intelligence. There are of course, sex differences in specific traits and the females have been found to be superior to males in linguistic ability and in tests of memory. Males have been found to be superior to females in mechanical ability and manual performance. But such studies appear to be superficial because most of the disparities are attributable to cultural influences and motivational factors working in individuals.

Psychological basis of Individual Differences

The analytical approach to individual differences emphasises the concept of differentiation to a great extent. It is assumed that the structure of human abilities and personality can be explained in terms of specific characteristics and traits. Various attempts have been made to account for the individual differences with reference to human abilities. Thustone's concept of primary ability has put forward a challenging notion of differentiation.

Burt has of course, attempted to take a middle course by presenting the theory of hierarchical structure of abilities while the U.S.E.F. investigation has found out as many as ten specific factors underlying this structure of human abilities. A few have pointed out some broad categories of factors like sensory and perceptual for taking into account the multi-dimensional nature of intellectual functioning. It is however to be admitted that the whole system of human functioning is interwoven to such an extent that it is difficult to isolate them in a limited framework. Individual differences, may also be observed in the personality structure. In other words, besides that cognitive differences, there are differences at the temperamental level. It is thus necessary to account for these differences in the affective domain and discover the relationship if any, between the two sectors. With the growing complexity of the science of psychology differentiation is emphasised more and more for practical purposes of selection and allocation. Yet one has to judge with an open mind if this is realistic or purely theoretical as a concept.

Sociological basis

The sociological basis of individual differences has gained much prominence in recent years. Among sociological factors which are considered to be very much important, cultural environment and social heredity deserve mention. The role of the home and group life in the development of personality has also been recognized. Thus this is a great concern for the educationists today.

Structure of Human Abilities

Attempts have been made to unfold the mysteries around human abilities. Theories of intelligence have been put forward by Spearman, Thorndike, Kelly and others accordingly.

Spearman and his followers had to modify the "Two factor Theory" to incorporate at least a few "Group Factors" which were supposed to be broader than the specific factor but less broad than "g" Thorndike suggests that there are three different types of intelligence viz., (a) abstract, (b) social, and (c) mechanical. He also stated that there are three dimensions of our intellectual activities including (i) aptitude, (ii) speed, and (iii) range or width.

Kelly in 1927 claimed to have established the three types of intelligence, namely (i) verbal, (ii) quantitative, and (iii) spatial. These three types of intelligence were shown by him as being independent of each other. Thus, in terms of Spearman's Theory, individuals would be found to differ in respect of only one type of intelligence, i.e. general intelligence. Thus the assessment of general intelligence may lead to the prediction of one's future attainments at least in the normal sphere of work. But in terms of Thorndike's or Kelly's finding there are three different types of intelligence in respect of which individuals may be found to differ. In other words, we have to investigate on the distinction between types, as follows:-

Abstract, Social and Mechanical }	According to Thorndike
Verbal, Quantitative and Spatial }	According to Kelly

The work of Stephenson and Spearman's "Two Factor Theory" showed that over and above "g" there was at least one broad group factor of a verbal nature. His analysis, however, did not preclude the existence of another broad grouping related to tests of only non-verbal character. Cox suggested of a factor (mechanical aptitude) after his experimental study on mechanical and routine assembly operations.

Koussy established "k" factor (space perception) found present in certain non verbal tests

Burt stated that the practical factor (F) was probably of a composite nature differentiating later on, in the course of a child's development, into two sub-factors, visuo-spatial (K) and mechanical (M), the former again maturing earlier than the latter.

In short, according to the English School of thought, all the factors, in addition to the general factor "g" should be regarded as so many broad 'group factors.' Then came Thurstone with his test of seven primary mental abilities viz.

Spatial ability, perceptual speed, numerical ability, verbal ability, word fluency, memory and response.

These abilities are primary as they are basic to any functioning of an individual and independent in the sense that they can enter separately or jointly into any functioning of an individual.

Another group of psychometricians headed by Thompson would hesitate to approve any of the above theories as they encourage minimising the number of common factors. They advocated another theory, viz. 'The Sampling Theory of Ability', which would attempt to explain all individual functioning in terms of interactions between innumerable traits or factors. Fleming nearly describes the last view when she says, "Mind is a rich, comparatively undifferentiated complex of innumerable influences."

The recent developments in factor analysis have, no doubt, influenced the concept of intelligence. Spearman in his later life recognised existence of a few broad group factors in addition to the "g" or general mental ability, while Thurstone in his subsequent findings recognised the existence of a second order "g" factor over and above his primary mental abilities. Many recent factorial studies show specific factor loadings in multiple and group factors after they have been rotated. The real difference between these views lies in the mode of approach and in the attitude towards the solution. While Thurstone and his followers would maximise the importance of primary abilities and minimise that of the second order "g" factor, Spearman's followers would do almost the reverse. In the American field of psychometry the list of factors representing primary abilities or aptitudes has continually expanded.

A set of factors or groupings has been shown to be fairly well established in the frequently used tests of abilities, as follows:-

(a) Verbal Comprehension

(b) Numerical Ability

(c) Abstract Reasoning

(d) Perceptual Speed

(e) Word Fluency

(f) Rote Memory

(g) Spatial Ability

(h) Mechanical Ability

(i) Musical Ability

(j) Artistic Ability and a few psychomotor factors like finger-dexterity, psychomotor co-ordination, etc.

Burt, after a thorough survey of the experimental work, suggested a hierarchical structure of human abilities consisting of the following successive levels:—

(a) General Intelligence, (b) Relation, (c) Association, (d) Perception, and (e) Sensation.

Burt's picture would look perhaps like the one below:-

(a) "g", the comprehensive general factor covering all cognitive abilities.

(b) Broader groupings on the higher relation level, e.g. apprehension of relations, aesthetic processes, etc.

(c) Broad group factors on the intermediate associative level covering different activities classified according to their form or content, e.g. memory, productive association, etc.

(d) Narrower factors at the 'perception' level.

(e) Factors at the sensation level.

The whole series would thus appear to be arranged at successive levels, the factors at the lowest level being the most specific.

Vernon seems to follow the middle of the road. According to him, the following structure would perhaps represent the intellectual and practical factors in psychological tests:

(a) "g" (general mental abilities)

(b) V:ed group and k:m group factors

(c) V:ed group subdivided into rote memory, verbal ability, etc., and k:m group subdivided into mechanical information, physical, aesthetic ability, psychomotor co-ordination, spatial ability, etc.

(d) Sub-division of the broad factors of the above category into narrower sub-factors.

(e) Crosscutting the two main groups of v:ed and k:m there are in addition a few more factors which may be described as belonging to 'speed' group.

When we look at both the American and British sets of psychological factors, we find that quite a number of them are common. The difference lies in the mode of approach. In one, these factors are treated as being more or less independent of each other, while in the other they are shown to form certain broad groupings in a connected whole.

A general outline of the realm of human abilities cannot be drawn unless the elements out of which the mind in compounded are discovered. We cannot hope to make successful predictions about an individual child until we know every side of his make-up. As Ahmavaara has put it: "All the possibilities created by the new differential method cannot presumably be seen as yet; a theoretical all-round picture is only beginning to take shape and connections between its different parts are still to be found. The methods are still very much in a state of evolution.

Besides the highly complex and controversial issue of identifying and naming the factors, we should note that all these factors *should be regarded primarily as categories for classifying mental and behavioural performances, rather than as entities in the mind or nervous system.

The findings of factorial research have, no doubt, important educational and vocational bearings. But opinions differ in regard to the usefulness of having test programmes of this or that type. It is being increasingly felt that educational and vocational guidance among adolescents is extremely difficult.

Individual Difference and attainment

The recent developments in psychology are more concerned with individual differences than with similarities. This is perhaps the outcome of a keen attempt at analysing human abilities and personality for the sake of selection and guidance. It is, however, strange that we are still confronted with the problem of mapping out the total personality of an individual in respect of its component parts. The psychometricians are optimistic on the future of such a thorough search for finding out all the individual differences. They have come to a general agreement in respect of structure of human abilities after a long pursuit. Intelligence has been regarded to occupy a pivotal place in the field. In spite of slight differences of opinion regarding the classification of intelligence, the nature and the function of this general ability has been accepted.

Three broad categories of intelligence have been identified in British school children at the time of entering secondary schools. Verbal, numerical and spatial abilities have been recognised as factors of intelligence, with their bearing on allocation of children. It is only recently that definite doubt has been expressed on the efficacy of the intelligence test in solving the allocation problem. This gesture leads to another controversial issue viz. what are the individual differences to be taken into account for the purpose of allocation? For a long time there was a tendency towards including personality qualities for a better prediction. But no systematic attempt has been made to enlist them on the basis of research evidence.

It appears that the British psychology clings to the traditional notion of accepting prima facie the human abilities more than dispositions for such purposes. Thus, aptitudes have been preferred to interest as a factor for determining one's course or vocation. The aptitude tests prepared for the purpose shows satisfactory results and they are being widely used at the moment for selection purposes. It is, however, accepted that the aptitudes involve some amount of ability and skill together with one inclination towards a specific area. Sporadic efforts reveal some amount of satisfaction as to the predictive value of aptitude tests particularly in science and technical courses. Mc Clelland's work supports the basis of selection by means of intelligence tests and at the same time hints at the possibility of including other tests for the purpose. Peel, Lambert and others confirmed that aptitude for technical drawing, etc., can be predicted by tests.

Peel points out that individuals differ widely in school attainments with respect both to quality and quantity. These attainments are the products of complex causes, viz. abilities, interests and opportunities. Feleming also observes, "neither the ability testing nor the aptitude testing have encouraged a belief in the possibility of exact prediction of the divisibility of human beings into discrete types."

In fact, there exists a large number of unknown variables influencing attainments. Vernon also assumes that personality factors like persistence, industriousness and interest contribute much towards one's success in almost all branches of learning.

The National Foundation of Educational Research, England in their first interim report of 1950 emphasised the need for identifying and assessing some of the non-examinable qualities of character and disposition. There are others like Himmelweit and Powell who stressed the importance of other characteristics such as ambition, speed and tendency to accuracy etc. Sanders also corroborates the previous result and refers to personality qualities and habits as important factors.

It would be thus clear that the individuals differ in various respects and a very few of them have till now received proper attention of the psychologists. Unfortunately, the problem of assessment of these qualities is so intricate that one would feel diffident in one's attempt to assess them accurately.

Very recently in his 'intelligence and attainment test,' Vernon has made a thorough survey of the present position of the intelligence test and pointed out the suitability of those tests for the purpose of any kind of selection. At the same time he has admitted with an open mind the limitation of these tests when he invites the attention to other factors like interest, relevant experience and opportunities, home background, physical strength and personality qualities.

Concluding Observation

No two persons are alike. If this be true, our interest would naturally be to find out the individual differences. In what respects do we differ from one another? In fact, human beings differ in many respects from one another. Abilities and aptitudes, vary from person to person apart from other factors.

What do we mean by abilities? Do they mean certain capacities or endowments with which people carry out their functions? Yes, human mind is made of a variety of potentialities and is too complex to be analysed. Also human mind functions at various levels of thinking, feeling (cognition, affection and conation).

The complex nature of human abilities has not been doubted. As a matter of fact, a wide range of capacities comprises the structure of human abilities. One may have a strong memory but a very poor reasoning. This indicates that our capacities are too diverse to be accounted for. For a systematic approach to this analysis psychologists have assumed that every individual has some fundamental power of adjustment to the outside environment. This power is known as the central ability or general ability. This is also known as intelligence in a broad sense of the term.

This term is, no doubt, very vague as it has various shades of meaning. Intelligence has been described in many ways. To a number of psychologists, intelligence is the capacity for abstraction. Here emphasis has been laid on the "Cognitive' aspect of mental ability, i.e. thinking and perceiving capacity. To some, intelligence is the power of problem solving while the capacity for reasoning has also been identified with intelligence by a few.

4

INTELLIGENCE AND ITS MEASUREMENTS —A Review

After a long search for a suitable definition of intelligence it has been established that it is the general ability which is manifest at various levels. It is like electricity which we find in every day use but which we can not determine.

It is really difficult to define intelligence. This is because of the complex nature of intelligence. The word intelligence goes back to Aristotle who tried to distinguish the emotional and moral functions from the cognitive and intellectual functions of our mind. Since then the structure of the mind has been questioned and the structural theories viewed and reviewed.

Various attempts to define intelligence have been made from different angles, viz. (a) the biological, (b) the psychological, and (c) the operational.

Charles Darwin and Herbert Spencer made the biological approach and pointed out the complexity of the higher brain centres and their bearing on the behaviour. According to this school of thought, intelligence has been regarded as an inherent capacity for profiting by experience, adaptation to environment and ability to learn.

Lloyd Morgan, Mc Dougall and Binet belong to this school. This approach to the definition of intelligence is not very acceptable for various reasons.

The biological conception in its original form refers to the modifiability of behaviour with increasing flexibility, which our intelligence test can hardly measure. Moreover, a follow-up study might give rise to a sceptical view of this approach because adaptation to the physical and social environment does not always indicate high intelligence or vice versa. Thus the term need be defined from various other angles, in order to explain the complexity of our behaviour in relation to environment. According to faculty psychology, our mind is composed of a number of major faculties, viz. knowing, feeling and willing. This faculty school went on extending their domain and included gradually various other powers of mind. Intelligence as a concept gradually developed and the question arose as to whether intelligence can be treated as a unitary faculty of the mind. As a corrolary, a second question arose: Is intelligence inborn or innate? Is it inherited from our ancestors or is it partly or wholly dependent on upbringing and education.

These questions have not been finally answered as yet, because intelligence is still an abstraction. It is only a mysterious, complex set of interpretations of "g". Rex Knight also supports Spearman by defining intelligence as the capacity for relational constructive thinking directed to the attainment of some end. Thorndike's attempt to reduce intelligence to the number of associations also deserves mention. It will be observed that psychological concepts of intelligence are being evolved out of confusion with a view to measuring intelligence in all its aspects. The most striking feature of these views is that all the functions overlap considerably and point to a general factor, difficult to be ignored. The different factors revealed by various mental tests constructed so far perhaps give out some partial aspects of intelligence. The theories of mental structure have been formulated by psychologists and various experimental approaches taken for identifying these factors.

Spearman's two factors theory recognised at last a dominant general ability accompanied by an amount of specific abilities, but the simple theory of hierarchy demonstrating generality did not explain the nature of the general factor of intelligence. Thomson pointed out this tendency towards over simplification expressed in Spearman's two factor theory. This is known as a sampling theory evolved by Thomson indicating the relativity of any general factor and any set of specific factors. These facts still await further exploration as neither the two factor theory helps to solve the problem of vocation or educational guidance calling for special aptitudes, nor the group factors of Thomson do account much of the variance of the test results. This controversy over general group and specific factors gave rise to Burt's concept of hierarchical organisation of mind based on the specific sensory-motor activities and tried to explain the mysteries underlying the concept of intelligence. In America a further development of the concept of intelligence was claimed by Thurstone. He challenged the overriding influence of a general factor of intelligence on all mental activities and discovered several primary group factors better known as "primary abilities."

It is thus clear that mere theoretical discussions about the nature of intelligence do not lead us anywhere. This is why Vernon has taken an operational approach to intelligence. He has dismissed the long-standing controversy by clarifying that intelligence is what intelligence tests measure. He supports his claim by an analogy. He says, "We can measure electricity without being able to define its precise nature and can put that to practical usage". He has gone further by saying that it is more consistent with the statistical evidence to think of intelligence as a fluid collection of abilities comprising the whole of mental life. It is a kind of average which cannot be pinned down to any single mental faculty, either by psychological or mental analysis. In his opinion the best definition we can give is rather simple, non-specific one such as all-round thinking capacities, or mental efficiency or general mental ability.

The Changing Concept of Intelligence

In recent years concepts of intelligence have undergone considerable changes. Hebb's neurological explanations are somewhat speculative, though he casts doubt on Gestalt psychologist's claim in explaining the intellectual behaviour of an infant through stages. An important feature of Hebb's view is that most perceptual schemata must be acquired at a suitable time, if further mental development is to be possible. Piaget also describes the stages and builds the sensory-motor schemata or patterns of response to external stimuli. He insists that intelligence is not one distinctive faculty nor can it be reduced to such. It is present in all adaptations of every living being. Behaviour in his opinion, becomes progressively more intelligent and the mental function more complex. It is thus a developmental concept of intelligences recently put forward by both Hebb and Piaget, influencing the modern views on intelligence.

Vernon classifies intelligence under three categories, viz, intelligence A, intelligence B, and intelligence C. Intelligence A is hypothetical only as we cannot directly observe or measure the genetic potentiality known as intelligence A. Intelligence B indicating the present mental efficiency represents the cognitive abilities developed in relation to suitable environmental stimulation. Intelligence C indicates the operational concepts of intelligence and is a later development.

Several significant points emerge from the discussion on these various concepts of intelligence. It has been clear that intelligence which can be observed in daily life or which is measured by tests should not be identified with the pure inborn natural capacity. If it were true that intelligence tests results depended almost wholly on innate ability, the I.Q. would be expected to remain constant throughout life. But unfortunately, a fluctuation has come to the notice of the psychologists in the I.Qs. under different circumstances. It has been seen that the effects of coaching and practice on intelligence tests brings out certain differences in I.Q. The effects of coaching, of course, seem to fade more rapidly than those of practice. Fortunately enough the fluctuation caused by either of the two is almost insignificant. It has also been observed that the home background has certain bearings on intelligence. It is really difficult to come to a definite conclusion as to the degree of the relative influence of heredity and environment on intelligence. It has been admitted, however, that the environment affects the child's intelligence to a certain extent. Burt's method of analysis yields a somewhat higher weight to heredity. In short, intelligence may be regarded as a product of both heredity and environment, though there may be some conflict regarding the relative weight of hereditary and environmental contribution.

Intelligence and Environment

Vernon in his book on Intelligence and cultural environment says. "It is the product of nature and nurture. In his opinion Intelligence test is no more than a sample of the kinds of skills we regard as intelligent. While intelligence A and Intelligence B refer to the genetic equipment and to the phenotype, there is another type of Intelligence which is non-genetic or rather acquire. Vernon adds Intelligence C to Hebb's dichotomy to indicate or refer to test-results as Intelligence. In 1951 the UNESCO consultants made the following concluding observation:-

"The Scientific evidence indicates that the range of mental capacities in all ethnic groups is so much the same. But Vernon does not entirely agree to this generalization. In this connection he comments "What they should have added is—there is no proof that innate mental differences do not exist."

Intelligence and its Measurement

What actually constitutes intelligence is a matter of controversy on which all psychologists do not seem to agree. In the beginning of this century, Stern defined it as the general ability by which a person can adjust his thinking to meet new requirements. Intelligence was thus a sort of master-key which is able to open, or atleast try to open the lock of all difficulties. Perhaps this fitted well with his theory of general factor of intelligence, for he held that a person's intelligence is able to work in every field. Patterson gave the corresponding behaviourists' definition, namely, a biological mechanism for integrating stimuli and producing adequate and unified response. It is really Stern's definition stated in other words. Terman who revised Binet's intelligence tests, thus working in verbal fields, defined intelligence as the capacity for abstract thinking. Wechsler, who worked with performance type of experiments, would define it as an ability to see through spatial (space) relationships. Perhaps, Colvin's definition as an ability to learn and adjust oneself to his environment seems a bit more impressive. We thus find intelligence being defined by some as general capacity to meet all situations as given by Stern, Patterson or Colvin, or as abilities in some specific areas, be it abstract as in the case of Terman or merely spatial as in the case of Wechsler. Thorndike would go to the other extreme denying its existence in any general field whatsoever and would admit only special abilities in specific fields. According to him, any comparison of general intelligence of a skilled computer, an expert mechanist, and a clever artist is impossible, for they have shown their abilities in various specific fields. Spearman would try to find a via media by admitting a general or common factor, which means an ability to meet difficulties of all sorts, whatever they may be, as well as a specific factor which means skills in several areas. Modern educators would, perhaps, improve upon this ideas by admitting that these specific skills again have two or more subdivisions. Abilities of a similar nature may be considered partly linked together and partly peculiar and isolated. They, would like to introduce group factors in intelligence and introduce what is known as the hierarchical theory of Parry, Vernon and Burt.

In the midst of so many conflicting definitions, it will perhaps be better if we try to find certain common qualities that are associated with the term intelligence. In the first place, it is a dynamic quality, namely a capacity to act. This action, of course, may not be visible in the shape of performance. It may be confined entirely in the realm of thinking, but is nevertheless directed to solve a difficulty, or to remove a certain obstruction. Secondly, it seems to be an innate capacity. Environment can develop it or make latent intelligence manifest, but environment can not produce intelligence within the person. Thirdly, though it helps us to accumulate knowledge, it should not be confused with knowledge itself. A person who has amassed a lot of knowledge may not necessarily be intelligent, he may not be able to adjust himself in a definite and novel situation, though perhaps the knowledge amassed may help him to find out a way some time. Fourthly, it should not be confused with such talents like memory or mechanical skill for both of these can be improved with practice, while intelligence is unaffected by practice. Lastly, though intelligence is one of the attributes of personality, yet there seems to be some distinction between what we call personality and what we call intelligence. Personality, has a distinct physical component. We can at the first sight pick out a person with a fine personality, and though with our later acquaintance we may not find him so attractive, yet our first favourable impression about him does not entirely die out. Personality, moreover, measures motivation, feelings, emotions, attitudes or interests, besides intelligence which merely measures efficiency or reactions.

The seat of intelligence is again a point of controversy. Psychologists of the last century held brain as the seat of intelligence and considered the size of the brain as a measure of intelligence. When it was found out that eminent writers like Anatole France, a Nobel Prize winner had a remarkably small size of brain, this theory was disproved. Modern psychologists have also failed to trace to what extent is quickness of reaction connected with intelligence. While skilled mechanists have generally a short reaction time, it has been seen that a clever artist or sometimes a novelist has a remarkable slow reaction time, and he takes more time to press the button in a Reaction Time Apparatus. Moreover, the rate of increase in the Reaction Time seems to be much more rapid than the so-called decline in intelligence, even when the intelligence is measured in the field of performance.

The modern theory of parry, Vernon and Brown would place intelligence at four distinct levels. At the base there is the strong undercurrent of General Intelligence which helps us to adjust ourselves into any new situation. Also are found major groups of abilities: Linguistic (Verbal), Quantitative (numerical), Ability to see space relationship (Spatial) and Ability to act (kinesthetic). Each of these abilities in turn may be subdivided into minor groups branching off into several specific capacities. While we have so far considered intelligence from a structural point of view, we may as well try to see it from a functional point of view. He has found three major components of intelligence namely:-

(a) An abstract capacity which helps us to deal with symbols, no matter whether these symbols refer to language or to quantities.

(b) Concrete capacity which helps us to deal with space relationships, as well as the ability to perform.

(c) Social capacity which helps us to deal with our social environment and gives us the ability to mix with other people. Shy and introvert persons if they are otherwise intelligent, will naturally give a good account of themselves in the first and in the second component, but will not perhaps do so well in the third. People who seem to impress us at the first sight and fail to impress us on closer acquaintance have probably the third capacity while their first two components may be sadly lacking.

Measurement of Intelligence : Binet's Test

Binet was faced with the task of grouping children who had the same acquired ability, but were endowed with different capacities. They were all illiterates but when a literacy campaign was started they proceeded at different rates, and it was an administrative necessity to group them so that each group would consist of persons having approximately the same abilities. He developed a test which did not require any linguistic ability beyond understanding and giving response. At first the test that was evolved in 1905, measured intelligence according to the number of correct answers, a person gave. This would perhaps solve the problem of granting persons admission to one class. Later as the scheme developed, persons came seeking admission to a higher class directly. The handicap of literacy alone should not debar a person to do so, for an intelligent person would be able to make up this deficiency in no time. It is so unfair to waste the time of a person of superior intelligence by putting him into a lower class. But how to find whether the claims put forward by an applicant for a higher class on the basis of superior intellect are justified. This can be done if we can devise tests suited to several stages of mental development. This was achieved by Binet when he developed his items according to grades or mental ages in 1908. Very soon a method was found to compare the intelligence of persons of different ages. The concept of I.Q. (Intelligence Quotient) was developed as revealed by his answers to intelligence test questions. The mental age thus found out by the test items was divided by his real or chronological age, and multiplied by hundred, to find out his I.Q. Stated symbolically,

$$\text{I. Q.} = \frac{\text{M.A}}{\text{C.A}} \times 100$$

Before applying a certain test to a group of persons and pronouncing the mental age of each individual, we must first ascertain its validity. With a degree of confidence the mental age groups have to be determined. Normally persons should reply according to their actual age norms (provided we work with a large number of children of each age group). For a subnormal person the response would be relatively poorer. It is, however, possible to put test questions to a large number of children of each group (which does not include exceptionally bright or dull children), and see whether their responses are according to expectations. Any question or item if not correctly replied by a large number of students in a certain age group should be treated as unsuitable for that group. This process is known as the validation and standardisation of the Test.

Although Binet's original test was meant for French students, its English counterpart was attempted both in England and in USA. In U.S.A. the work done was more outstanding. Terman went through an elaborate process of standardisation and modification, and ultimately developed two versions of the test. The advantage of the two versions is obvious. We may apply one version and get the results, then we may apply the second version for confirmation. We may thus find out the reliability of the test of intelligence. Each of the series, L. and M contains 129 questions divided into mental age groups as follow:-

(a) Six questions for each half-yearly period from 2 to 4-1/2 years. This is done because the development at this period is more rapid than at a later age. A correct answer naturally adds to the mental age by a month at this stage.

(b) Six questions each for early periods from 5—14, a correct answer at this stage gives a credit of two months.

(c) Eight questions suited to average adult, where credit for a correct answer is still two months.

(d) Six questions for each of three groups called by him as superior adults I, II and III, while the credit for a correct answer in superior adults III is five months. The longer period provided in higher age is backed by the theory that the growth of intelligence slows down as age advances.

The remaining 7 questions are given as alternatives in different age groups. When a person answers all the questions, his mental age will be 22 years and 10 months, at which age growth of intelligence (as measured by the test) stops.

A question may arise as to what will happen to a person, say 46 years old, answering all questions correctly. Evidently he can not do anything better than scoring a mental age upto 22 years and 10 months. If his achievement is divided by his chronological age and multiplied by 100, his I.Q. will not be above 50. Evidently, he is being penalised for his age. To avoid this, Terman proposed a modification of the real or chronological age.

For administration of the test, Terman would not ask the experimenter to put all the questions to every child. He would make a rough guess of what the mental age of the child is likely to be, (for mental age above eight, perhaps administration in vocabulary item of the test may be helpful, as answer in that test would indicate the rough mental age). He would then put to the child all the questions set for age. If the child is able to answer all the questions, he will be given the questions suited to the next higher age. Other-wise he will be given the questions suited to the next lower age. In this way, the basal age or the highest age upto which the child is able to answer all the questions will be determined. The credit in years and months suited to the basal age will be given to him to start with. Then he will begin answering questions from those mental age groups where his answers will be only in parts of each mental age group. For each answer he will be given the credit for the corresponding months (One, two, four or five as the case may be) till he comes to an age where he is unable to answer a single question. At this point, the administration of the test will stop. His total credit in mental age will be the basal age plus the sum of monthly credits he has earned. The mental age so obtained, when divided by the chronological age (actual age upto thirteen, corrected age between thirteen and sixteen, and multiplied by 100 will give the person's Intelligence Quotient.

Terman found with a very wide administration of his test that intelligence of different age groups is more or less normally distributed. Roughly about two thirds of the entire group was found to have an intelligence quotient somewhere between 85 and 119. For convenience, however, he took the demarcation lines at points 110, 120 and 140 on the right side of the normal line and at points, 90, 80, 70 and 60 on the left (normal line being 100, which represents the points where mental and chronological ages are equal). Terman found that about 60% of the people are distributed between 90 and 110. This is according to him, the score of persons of average intelligence. Between 110 and 120 on one side and between 80 and 90 on the other, there are about thirteen per cent on each. The former he will call high and the latter low. Between 120 and 143 are 6.75% cases whom Terman will call superior and beyond 140 are rare persons. About 25% of these he will call genius. On the other side, between 60 to 80 there are about 60% cases who may be called dull or morons, and below 60 are the remaining 1% who are idiots or imbeciles. Thus the test not only measures intelligence, but can be used for clinical diagnosis of morons and imbeciles. Mental abnormalities like neurosis and psychosis cause a regression. Such persons though physically mature, behave like children. They thus register an abnormally low mental age, and this fact added to other clinical observations would support the findings that they are of abnormal mind.

There have been various adaptations of this test in India notably by Sohan Lal and Bhatia at Allahabad, Kamath in Bombay and recently in Calcutta University. They are thus available in at least four Indian languages, Hindi, Gujarati, Marathi and Bengali. But these seem to have been standardised on a limited population, and perhaps are not yet complete for all age groups with two parallel forms as in the case of Terman. The application of Terman's Test in India, however, has its limitation, not only because of the language handicap, (which gives an additional advantage to a person whose command over the English language is better) but because of its cultural saturation. Sohan Lal's adaptation may be all right for U-P, but may not suit other parts of India.

Point Scale Group Tests

Binet Test or its Terman Revision, is an individual test in which each person is tested separately. Though it allows a certain amount of flexibility, yet it is very time-consuming and expensive. To prevent this, certain group tests like Army Alpha have been evolved. They may contain some true and false items and the subjects may find out which of them are true and which false. Another group may contain several plausible answers out of which the subjects may be asked the one best suited. A third group may need a rearrangement of items, a fourth group may need simple mathematical computation, and so on. For each correct answer a score may be given, and suitable corrections may be made to avoid guess work. The test resembles an objective test with the difference, that it has been verified as suitable, and it is again given to a number of persons belonging to several age groups. The score for each age-group is obtained. These scores are then distributed over a hundred point scale separately for each age group. This provides us with a suitable measuring stick with which we can assess any individual ability, according to the performance of the individual in terms of the accomplishment of the normal persons of his own age group. A person's score corresponding to sixty points in the scale of performance of his own group means that fifty-nine persons of his age group selected at random will get points lower than what he has scored in the test. His rating or percentile rank will then be sixty. This is known as the point scale and it is an average. A person gets a percentile rank of 50 instead of 100 in the age scale.

Semi-performance Scales : Wechsler Bellevue Test

Wechsler has evolved in the Bellevue University a combined test of eleven groups of items six of which (Nos. 1, 2, 3, 4, 5, and 11) are of the verbal type and may be applied to the literates and the other five of the performance type which are applicable both to the literates and illiterates. Both the categories have been standardised separately as well as together. In fact, Wechsler's aim at evolving the test seems to be two fold.

He wanted to find out objectively whether ability known as variable intelligence is interrelated to abilities in the performance type of activities. If the correlations are high, it will prove that it measures intelligence correctly, and the scores would be the most general measures of intelligence. It would thus justify Wechsler's definition of intelligence.

He wanted to develop further scale by which adult intelligence could be measured. Binet's Test or its Terman Revision can register mental age only upto 22 years and 10 months. What happens afterwards? Does the adult intelligence remain stationary or does it decline are the pertinent questions one may ask ? Wechsler has tried to answer this.

The Bellevue scale of intelligence is somewhat in between the Terman's or Binet's conception of intelligence quotient based on the consideration of mental ages and the point scale for finding a percentile rank of a person's achievement compared with his own age group. Wechsler would first get the score by administering the entire test to his subjects (ages between 10 and 50) and for the convenience of marking will allot points for a correct answer which will generally be one and rarely upto three (as in block tests). He will also allow time credit for quick and successful answers given before time and this will also be upto three in case of exceptionally quick and correct answers. Now some of the groups contain easier items and some harder, their weightages in predicting intelligence can not, therefore, be considered same. Wechsler would, therefore, give added value to certain items according to their importance in predicting intelligence, and reduce the values of others. Thus the weighted score for intelligence will be calculated.

The weighted scores of an individual are then compared with the achievements of the person's own age group to find out his position according to a method which resembles the point scale.

But Wechsler does not write his answers on a simple point scale. He takes up Binet's conception of intelligence and holds that median intelligence should be rated at 100. He, however, holds that normally fifty, out of every hundred persons should be showing the average intelligence (as opposed to Terman's 60%) and these should be between the scores 90 and 110. Wechsler thus takes 100 as the mean and 90 and 110 as plus and minus P.E. distances according to statistical concepts.

Wechsler has found a fair degree of interrelationship between the performance and verbal intelligence, and his scale is able to measure intelligence in terms of I.Q. (his own concept of it) for all age groups from 10 to 50 years. It has the disadvantage, like Binet's test in being individual and its administration is both expensive and time-consuming.

WAIS is an extension and modification of Wechsler Bellevue Intelligence scale. Important changes have been made in the directions for administering and scoring the tests. Some items have been dropped and some new items have been added. The WAIS norms were based on groups considered representative of U.S. adults.

Norms were developed for each of seven age groups ranging from 46 to 64 years.

When assessing the effectiveness of Intellectual ability in an adult, one is primarily interested in two kinds of comparisons: how the individual compares with his age peers and how he compares with those who are at the base of mental development.

The WAIS intelligence Quotient (IQ), whether based on Verbal. Performance or Full Scale is obtained from a direct comparison of the subjects test results with those of persons in his chronological age group.

The WAIS standardization sample was chosen with exceptional care to insure its representativeness. The verbal, performance and full scale scores can be expressed in terms of I.Qs. with a mean of 100 and an SD of 15.

Other Intelligence Tests

The tests of intelligence of a simpler type are those of Maze learning or Draw a Person Test. These measure spatial relationship or only one aspect of intelligence. Koh's block measures both spatial relationship and ability to perform. Pegboard judges only performance, but Seguin's formboard measures spatial relationships as exhibited by patterns and performance ability. These tests thus measure only one or at best two aspects of what we call intelligence.

More complicated types of performance tests have been evolved like Army Beta test which like Army Alpha is a group performance test in India. The psychological Bureau, Allahabad has evolved Bhatia's Battery which is an adaptation of several tests including, Alexander's

Pass along test and others. This has been standardised and can be used as a performance test suitable under Indian conditions.

One great objection that is often raised against these tests are that they are not entirely culture-free. They give some additional advantage to the groups whose socio-cultural background represents that of the test maker. Some critics have indeed asserted that the tests constructed provide a justification for the higher socio-economic groups to obtain more favourable treatment in the matter of educational opportunities for their children. This is perhaps a rather strong and uncharitable remark to make against the use of test. The cultural saturation is always a strong limitation which we may not always be conscious of and this sometimes handicaps one in constructing a test.

It must be noted, however, that to meet this objection some culture-fair tests have been evolved where the cultural saturation is at least perceptibly reduced. International group mental test of Dodd is a pictorial test prepared according to common culture of human beings and in co-operation with the anthropologists. It includes Code Substitution, Block Counting, Maze Tracing, Series of completion and arrangement of Items. International Performances Test is another which has been revised in 1948. It eliminates instruction altogether. Each test begins with a few easy tasks to be performed which are self-educative. Among the tasks included are matching of identical colours, Block design, Foot print recognition spatial relations, classification of animals etc. Tests are arranged in year level from 2 to 18. Cattell's culture fair tests are available at three age levels, Scale I for 4-8, II for 8-12 and III for higher ages (up to Terman's Superior Adults).

Raven's Progressive Matrices Tests have been designed to measure the 'g' factor of intelligence. It consists of sixty matrices or abstract designs from each of which a part has been omitted. The Subject chooses the missing part from six or eight given alternatives. The items are grouped into five series each of which consists of twelve matrices of increasing difficulty but similar in principle. The earlier series require chiefly accuracy of discrimination, the later includes analogies, permutation, alteration of pattern and other logical relations. The scoring is done on a point scale and Raven has worked out percentile norms for all ages 5-14 in half yearly intervals and then form 20 to 65 in five year intervals. Testing in Argentina has proved significant saturation with culture. But Green working in Ceylon has found that it is not entirely culture free though favouring certain professions rather than others Mat-weavers of Ceylon who work with patterns got better scores than college graduates. Recently, an easier and coloured version of Raven's test suitable for 5-11 years have been made both in book and in board. The subject is to choose the right piece rather than choose the correct completion. Its ceiling value seems to be low for even children of average ability score in India.

Although we seem to know what is intelligence, we can not like many other terms, define intelligence in a way that may be acceptable to all. Different psychologists have tried perhaps to measure the different aspects of intelligence and have emphasised one aspect or other. We can not deny that one shows the average in his performance or actions even when he is confronted with difficulties of a different nature. This points to a general ability factor in intelligence. But one cannot at the same time overlook that while some people are clever in verbal responses, others are good in number responses or performance ability.

Spatial relationships may not show themselves so well in verbal responses. This points to the intelligence being somewhat specific, running into some groups. We can not at the same time deny that in addition to group ability some persons show remarkable cleverness in some specific area of either verbal, spatial, number of performance aspect. Thus we have to consider intelligence to be consisting of several factors or levels, eg. general, group and specific.

Measurement of intelligence is necessary, for obvious reasons, to group children or adults of the same intelligence range so that they may be given guidance or instruction accordingly. This is possible, provided one can devise suitable tests. Such tests may be either individual with advantage of flexibility and scope for adjustment to fatigue or boredom of the subject. They may again be devised along on age scale where questions are divided according to different groups and the successful answer gives the subject a credit in years or in months. This finally settles the Mental age of the subject and when we divide this by the subject's real or chronological age we can get a measure by which we are able to compare the intelligence of other persons. We may have to adjust the real age so that the I.Q. may not be inflated. As the age scale provides not one but several tests, it is also called a 'battery type test'. Besides an age scale, there is a point scale in which the same test is given to all subjects. The test may contain several groups of items, but their administration is common to all groups. The test of this type is thus an 'Omnibus' pattern. Here the performances of normal persons of several age groups must be collected and spread over a hundred point scale. To fix up the position of a new person, all that we have to do is to compare his performance with others of his own age group and to find out where he stands on a hundred point scale. Evidently more intelligent persons would stand high in the list and the position of less intelligent ones will be low in the scale.

While Binet's test or its Terman and Merrill Revision, measures verbal intelligence along an age scale, the Army Alpha measures it on a point scale. The former is an individual and the latter a group test. Wechsler Bellevue Test is a semiperformance test, measuring both verbal and performance types but either part can be used separately or both together. The fact that two parts correlate well, proves some connection between verbal intelligence and an intelligence of the performance type. Wechsler has devised a scale in measuring intelligence according to the performance of a subject being compared to his own age group, but he makes adjustments by taking probable error value to bring it to a form similar to Intelligence Quotient of Binet.

There are many other tests of Intelligence which have been devised, some of which like the Form Board, Maze Learning, Draw a Preson Test, or Peg Board Test measure limited aspects of intelligence. Others have been so constructed as to give objective measurements of intelligence in any cultural context. Among the latter, may be mentioned the names of Dodd's International Group mental Tests, Leiter's international performance Test (Devised in Battery pattern), Cattell's culture-free Test and Raven's progressive matries. While reducing the influence of culture one can not, however, say with certainty that these tests are entirely culture-free.

5

PERCEIVING AND THINKING

What is perception ?

To a man in the street there is hardly any difference between perception and mere looking. To a scientist, however, perception has a special significance. It means receiving impressions through any of the senses including sight, hearing, smell, touch or taste. In a psychological sense it further involves two things namely to receive the sensation and to interpret them. Besides good senses and effective sensations there must be a proper span of attention and motivation for learning.

Thomas Reid distinguished between mere sensation and perception. In an ordinary sensation, the sense organs receive certain impressions and there the matter ends. In perception, there is not only a stimulus but also some meaning, which can be derived by a sense of awareness or knowledge of the subject. We may for instance see a red flower and its redness and roundness are apparently sensations though they too need previous experience or acquaintance and in that sense they are also perceptions. But to recognise that flower as a rose, a previous knowledge of the details of the property of the flower is needed. Brown holds that perception is really grasping of relationships. We perceive not merely similarities, but the differences from other objects to establish peculiarities. Before we have perceived the red flower as the rose we have not only noticed how it resembled our previous impressions of roses, but at the same time how the particular flower differed from other red flowers. Wundt and James hold that perception combines a number of sensory elements. When we perceive a rose, for instance, we consider not merely the colour and shape, but its smell as well. The sensation of pleasure that a cup of tea offers is a combined sensation of its warmth and its flavour which is a blending of two more sensations namely smell and taste. Thus touch, smell and taste are all involved in it.

Cattell working on attention span found that adults can apprehend six to eleven objects at a time, provided the objects are not too big. The average is generally eight. If, however, items are bundled into groups more can be perceived. An ordinary person can note as many as thirty letters provided these letters make a meaningful sentence.

Urban Schis and Necker found that our attention fluctuates. We can test this fact ourselves through many experiments. On looking at cube the surface ABCD appears in front for a while, and PQRS at the back. At other times PQRS may appear to be in front, ABCD at the back. What is true for sight is true for other senses also.

William James and Edward Titchener hold that when we pay attention to some thing, we bring it to a focus and other things go into the margin of our attention. Morgan studied the problem of distraction. Subjects in a certain experiment were made to learn a certain code on a kind of type writer by punching certain signs. While they worked bells were rung. For a short while in the earlier part, the work slowed down showing the effect of distraction. After a while, as the subjects got used to the sound, the distraction did not have much effect on their perception or attention, and they worked at their usual speed. Now the bell was suddenly stopped. Curiously enough work slowed down again. The explanation is quite simple, formerly the bell was causing distraction, but the persons got used to them. After a while it is the stoppage of the sound, that caused distraction. Titchener also found that the size, motion, colour or as a matter of fact any stimulus which can stand prominently against the background of experiences, serves as a factor to control attention.

Cattell, working on the reaction time apparatus, found that our attitude or expectation influences the speed of our reaction. Some subjects were asked to concentrate on the response they should make when they saw the light. After a while they were asked to concentrate on the stimulus itself. It was found that they worked faster in the former case.

Watt, working on controlled association, found that when a subject was told to give the opposite of each word, he usually adjusted himself to this unusual situation by practising a few cited before-hand. While he had thus practised, the perception of opposites became automatic.

These experiments threw much light on perception. They showed that factors like distraction are relative to the situation, we get used to. In case of opposites, we adapt ourselves to a situation to be ready to receive the stimulus and to perceive. Perception thus needs a preparation.

Gestalt Theory and Perception

Wertheirmer, Kohler and Koffka have held that our experience is a total process in which parts can not be easily differentiated or analysed. We perceive a rose as such, we can not isolate either the colour or the shape and say that this is rose. Even in case of its smell, we can not isolate the several items that blend together to give us the peculiar smell of a rose. A cup of tea of a peculiar blend is perceived as a whole and declared delicious. We can not break it into its elements of taste smell and other things that make its flavour.

Kohler trained a hen in such a way that when she picked up grains from a grey paper, she was permitted to eat them. When she picked up the grains from a white paper, she was driven away. By and by, she became so used to this situation, that the hen would pick up only from the grey paper. After a time the white paper was removed, and the grains were spread over two papers, one black and other grey. Now it was seen that the hen went straight for the black paper, thus showing that what the hen perceived was not the particular paper which was grey, but the entire situation, namely the comparatively darker part of the two bits of papers.

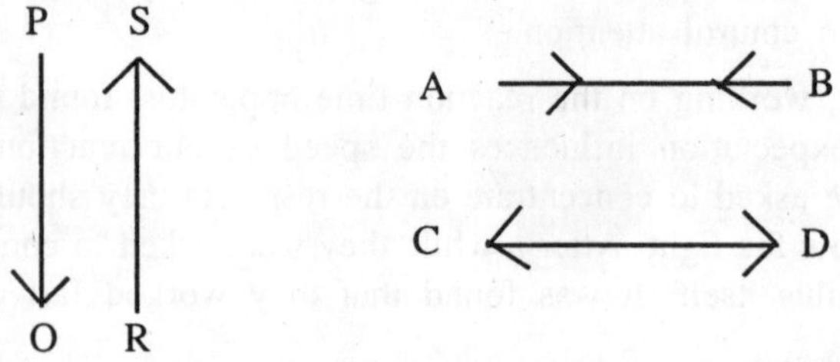

An illustration of the false deception, how our eyes can deceive us is shown in the above figures. The lines AB and CD are of equal length, and yet CD appears longer, because of the projection pointing outwards. The line PQ and RS are parallel and yet they appear approaching each other because of the trim transversal lines approaching each other.

In these two illustrations also, the total situation affects us. Perception of depth is caused by perspective lines converging at a vanishing point. This was found and used first by the clever artist De Vinci. Here too the total situation, the relation of a thing with regard to its background gives us the idea of the depth. Descarte's discovery that changes in the eye help us to gauge the distance, looks at this issue from an organic stand-point, but this kind of accommodation of the eye itself is an evidence that we perceive things together and that our eyes try to accommodate all.

It is on this basis that Whetstone constructed stereoscope in 1838. Two pictures that were presented to the right and to the left eyes were not exact carbon copies, but they had slight differences only. It is by accommodation to these differences, that the eyes get a vivid impression of the depth. This fact thus objectively shows not only the accommodation of the eyes but also a tendency of reaction towards the total situation of the Gestalt.

Thinking and thought process : Behaviourists' View

Upto the time of Wundt, it was believed that images are absolutely necessary before thinking can start, and that our thoughts go in terms of sensations, images, and feelings. Binet and Oswald Kulpe tried to disprove this but it was Buhler who succeeded in giving an experimental evidence. Buhler tried to analyse the thinking which evolved when a subject was confronted with a paradox. The apparently impossible things in a paradox should at once strike the subject had he used his past images, but he found that a subject was made to think and draw conclusions thus showing that an image is not necessary. Likewise, a subject may be made to think and draw conclusions when he hears a fable. Certainly, in this case there are no images, for no one has heard an animal talk; yet there is thinking.

Robert Woodworth's Publication : 'Imageless Thought' also gives evidence of sensations not affecting our thought process though evidence of such sensations received in the past may be provoked deliberately by introspection. Based on these and on his own experimental evidence, Wundt held that the core of thinking process was merely a conscious perception of relationship and not necessarily of past images.

Watson put forward the viewpoint of the behaviourists on this subject. According to him, thinking is nothing but talking to one's ownself in a manner that no sound is being produced. Sometimes, many of us, especially children, think aloud. We generally give up this process as we grow older, because we are afraid of being ridiculed. Watson believed that thinking can go in terms of any muscular experience. Certain deaf and dumb individuals, he found, try to think by moving their hands, thus showing that they are merely repeating the mode of expression that they otherwise use. Under normal circumstances, as we speak, these individuals express themselves, by show of hand. While thinking they are using the same method, or in one sense they are thus thinking aloud.

Experiments by other psychologists have, however, failed to reveal any significant relationship between thinking and movement of vocal muscles, perceptible or otherwise, which would have proved this theory.

Several hypothesis have been put forward. According to the motor theory, thinking is something like muscular action. The supporters of this viewpoint have not, however, been able to give sufficiently convincing experimental evidence.

In 1939, Berger reported that he had found the existence of an electric current with about ten oscillations (to and fro movement) per second when a person is made to think. This he called 'Brain Waves'. Berger found this by placing two metallic rods or electrodes on the surface of a person's skull. These were connected with a Galvanometer or an electrical measuring instrument while a person was thinking. Berger's followers have claimed that the intensity of waves increases as a person's mental age increases. Unfortunately, not many researches have been carried out in this direction. All that one can say at the present moment that when sufficiently convincing evidence is available, this may change our present trend of psychology and establish once more that thinking is a process in which brain alone is involved. At present, however, we are not in a position to assert this so convincingly.

Thinking Process in terms of Gestalt Theory

Gestalt psychologists have introduced 'insight' to describe the thought process. Persons, it is held, grasp relations unconsciously and the solution of the problem strikes one suddenly. Kohler found many examples of insight in apes. If food is hung from the ceiling of a box, the apes could pile up boxes to reach it and some time they would pull the food down by attaching one stick to another, if a single stick would prove a bit too small. This attachment would be conveniently done. These do not show a mere chance reaction as has been claimed in the solution of maze problems, when an animal was to run a maze to procure its food, more or less blindly. Kohler held that even in the maze problem entire relationship was surveyed before the problem was solved. Tolman and others built and elevated transparent maze wall so that a rat could see the type of maze they run through. Within the maze there were two paths, one shorter than the other. The fact that 90% of rats choose the shorter path was a clear evidence that their choice was not a matter of chance, but a result of deliberate insight into relationships. When however a hurdle was kept along the shorter path, the rats chose the longer path which did not have the hurdle. This is again the result of the perception of the total relationship.

Hunter kept three boxes. Only one of them did contain some food and this was momentarily lighted. Children were told to find their food from one of the boxes. Perhaps at the start, they made a few mistakes, but after a while, they could reach the right box without any mistake. That this perception of the right box associated with lighting, was proved by switching on the light to a wrong box. Then the children went to the wrong box invariably for they had grasped the relationship of the box to the light.

Reasoning

Reasoning is an orderly or logical sequence in which thinking follows. John Dewey has established five distinct steps involved in a reasoning process:-

1. There must be a problem, some perplexity or difficulty. If everything runs smoothly where is the need for an individual to exert ?
2. We must be able to locate or define the difficulty. If then the situation is so complex that we can not make head or tail out of it, we are likely to give up attempts of solving it, and get desperate. There will be no attempt at reasoning, for there will be no attempt of problem solving.
3. While reasoning, we try to put forward a hypothetical solution. This is only a tentative or a trial solution, and while putting forward, we are conscious that in the light of further investigation, we may be required to modify or alter it.

4. We examine and develop this hypothesis in the light of the given conditions and see whether the hypothesis meets all our requirements.
5. We finally verify our hypothesis or put it to actual test to see whether it actually fulfils all the conditions. If it does not, we may have to repeat the process involved in steps (3), (4) and (5) with a new hypothesis.

The five steps indicated in the above may not occur in the order given, though it generally does so, but it is essential that all the steps must be involved in the process which we call reasoning.

As an example we may take the case of a man observing a long pole projecting horizontally from the upper deck of a boat. For an observer it may be a problem as to find out why is it put at all ?

On attempting to locate the difficulty, the man notices that the pole is horizontal, which at once rules out the possibility of its being a flagpost. The observer is now confronted with two hypotheses, it may either be a wireless post or the pole erected to point out the direction to the steerman. On testing the first hypothesis, he concludes that had it been a wireless post it would have been pitched higher up on the top of the pilots cabin, for higher the pole the better will be its transmitting and receiving power. If on the other hand, the pole is meant for pointing out the direction to the steerman, it would not be pitched so high as to obstruct the pilot and would be just high enough to be visible from the steerman's place. The former hypothesis, therefore, not being able to withstand verification is rejected.

Two types of Reasoning:

Reasoning may be of two types. After we have already established a law we want to prove the conclusion for a particular case. This is known as deduction and is used in our geometrical theories. For example, we take the particular case of two triangles whose corresponding sides are equal. Applying the general fact that in such cases, the triangles become congruent, we prove the congruency of this particular case using the general law.

Yet all our reasonings are not of this type. At times we generalise and get a common underlying truth out of the study of a number of particular cases. This common truth in the concept and the process is known as induction. A child's concept of an animals is, for instance formed out of a study of a number of concrete experiences of dogs, cats, goats, rabbits, rats from which he might have formed the common and essential feature which he called the concept of an animal. Having drawn this concept, the child may use it to compare new cases and thus applies this inductive knowledge to deduction. Induction and deduction are, therefore, complementary processes and are by no means exclusive. When a new problem confronts us, we certainly try to find its solution in terms of our past experiences, and to solve the novel and particular case with some similar past experience or concepts. But after all, these concepts or general ideas are built out of a study of a number of isolated experiences which are grouped together for facility of remembrance.

Summary

We find that perception is not mere seeing but is connected with experience with all the senses. It has several characteristics. It is no doubt, selective, for we react to one aspect of the total environment at a time, which we focus our attention for the moment. But at the same time we are not indifferent to the total situation which serves as the background for our observation. Perception is moreover, a meaningful process. Our past experiences and our present mental set up are both connected with it. Sometimes several sensations from several sense organs are blended together to give a meaning. How many separate items can be comprehended together, depends on the nature and difficulty of the items as well as on the mental age of the learner. Further, it depends also on the fact whether the items can be grouped together or not. Distraction prevents perception, but what we call distraction is really a chance in the situation one gets used to. If a person gets used to noise, it is quietness that will become distracting. When we expect a thing to happen in a certain way, our mind gets adjusted to this situation and our responses become automatic.

What constitutes thinking, has given rise to many conflicting theories. In many cases, thinking may be as the behaviourists claim it to be, mere talking to oneself, which may or may not be backed by past images. Perhaps under such circumstances, it may depend on conscious perception of relationships.

Yet it is not clear whether thinking takes place in the brain alone as Berger claims it to be. His experiments have been carried on a limited scale. We are not yet in a position to state whether it would give us a general truth applicable to all cases of thinking. It is undeniable that at least at times, thinking is based on the result of the perception of the total relationship. In such cases the final solution comes out as flash as if by insight, but it is really an outcome of the analysis of the total situation going on within the mind as the Gestalt psychologists claim.

In more complex cases, we have to reason out in a logical manner which involves not merely a perception of relationship, but also that of locating it. After locating the difficulty, the mind puts forward a trial solution or hypothesis, which is put to test and which needs verification. If the hypothesis does not stand verification, it is rejected and a new hypothesis is called for. If it stands verification, it is accepted.

The two processes of reasoning, deduction or applying general truths to a particular case, or induction or building up a general concept by studying a number of particular difficulties are really complementary and one can seldom be treated as exclusive of the other.

Concluding Observation

Perception is dependent upon the impressions made upon our senses by different objects or conditions around us. It involves a meaning or a recognition of these objects. Sensation is a step towards perception. It is a question of not only how things are, but how things appear which is important in perception. In other words, the character of the perception is more important than the character of objects that are perceived. It has been admitted that consciousness is one of the important conditions of perception. The phenomenological experience of an object is dependent on one's own organism, so the phenomenology has to depend upon the two sides of the same process. It does not cover the whole of experience.

Recent evidence supports the views that perceptual organisation is related to experience. The process of perception itself is susceptible to social influences. This is also evidenced from various research findings. Besides, the operation of rewards and punishment, personal needs and emotional states influence the way in which an individual perceived. The experiences help one to acquire meanings and thus they become more dominant in the perceptual field. In other words, the patterning of impressions gradually leads to organised percepts.

The organism and the environment offer an extremely crowded perceptual field and selection of certain stimuli is one of the basic questions involving perceptions. Clinical evidence indicates that much depends upon the nature of stimulation. If the stimulation is intense, perception is enriched. As mentioned before, the nature of experiences determines to a large extent the behaviour pattern of an individual in the formation of an attitude towards a particular object. Similarly, the culture context has got an important bearing on the formation of percepts. Communication, language, symbols and perception are inter-related to some extent. The complexity of perceptual process is significant particularly when we consider the process within the context of social situation and social interaction. Some of the experiments with chimpanzees go to prove that the response to a stimulus depends upon one's perception of the object. The relationship of the objects to the perceiver determines the perceptual process which depends upon past experience and action. A knowledge of the learning process is relevant for understanding the part played by culture in the specification of perception. Such knowledge includes an awareness of biological conditions basic to learning and understanding of the operation of repetition, generalisation, transfer and dominance.

There are few questions which are important in this connection:

1. What are the contents and properties of an individual's perception? What determines these properties? while we perceive, our perceptual world is dependent on the nature of the physical objects which surround us. It is also much dependent upon objects and events not immediately present. It is a complicated way in which we perceive the world and how we perceive the world is a product of memory, imagination, fantasy as well as our sense experiences. In other words, certain cognitive structures and substructures emerge out of this process. In the field of social psychology, various problems, emerge in connection with cognitive organisation. To get a good description of man's cognitive world is extremely difficult, and various errors creep in and create confusion.

On a review of the psychological aspects of perception it appears that here are two major determinants of perception. There are structural, as well as functional factors involved in perception. By structural factors are meant those which are derived solely from the nature of physical stimuli and the neural effects they evoke in the nervous system of the individual. The functional factors of the perceptual organisation are those derived primarily from the needs, moods, past experience and memory of the individual. The experiments performed by Bruner and Goodman show that differences in perception of the two groups of children asked to estimate the size of the coins are mainly due to the effect of need upon their perception. The greater the individual need for socially valued objects, the more marked will be the operation of behavioural determinants. Another experiment by Lewin, Chain, and Murphy illustrates the importance of functional factors operating in perception. The more important part in the perceptual process is played by the inter-relation between structural and functional factors. The piecemeal approach does not offer a complete picture of the various aspects of perception. It is, therefore, important that perception should be approached from the standpoints of both an experimental psychologist and a social psychologist. With a view to analysing the nature and process involving perception, it will be better if the following propositions are formulated:-

1. The perceptual and cognitive field in its natural state is organised and meaningful. Man is an organising animal and any fact we experience will be organised into some sort of meaningful whole. This tendency towards organisation is a universal characteristic of the cognitive process.

2. Perception is functionally selective. In every day life, the physical stimuli we are exposed to are various. It is, therefore, important that selection of certain stimuli will have to be made for integration and specific organisation of our cognitive field. It is true that objects that play the major role in the organised perception serve an immediate purpose of the perceiving individual.

3. The perceptual and cognitive properties are determined in large measure by the properties of structure of which it is a part, It is a fact that experience in the natural state is organised and meaningful, but our cognitive field does not consist of completely independent organised structure. In other words every perception is embedded in an organisation of other percepts. Thus, each of these cognitive structures can be broken down into several relative sub-structures. It is the interrelationship among the structures and substructures of the cognitive field which should be determined for the understanding of any perception.

Illustration from simple visual perception will indicate the importance of contrast and assimilation in understanding the substructure of a major structure as related parts and wholes. This general whole-part principle has so many extensions. As a result, the formulation of whole-part principles proves sounder in terms of constancy of the cognitive field. If there were no object constancy in our perceptual life, all objects of our world would look radically different every time. The whole-part principle can be better explained in terms of frames of reference.

The term frame of reference is simply used to denote the functionally related factors which operate at the moment to determine the particular properties of a psychological phenomenon such as perception. Sheriff has demonstrated the importance of major concepts in social psychology. Nelson and MeGravey had shown the importance of phenomenon of relativity in the perceptual field.

For every organised perception the individual is attuned or adapted to the central stimulus in the light of his needs and judgment.

4. Final proposition indicated that certain perceptions are organised together with other perceptions to make up a single cognitive structure. The common structure is influenced by the objects or events, by contiguity of space and time or resemblance. This is a very important proposition so far as its social implications are concerned.

Differences in social behaviour among men reflect differences in the cognitive structure which is dynamic. There is a constant organisation and re-organisation in the perceptual structure which takes place with reference to the needs and attainment of the goal. The cognitive process of re-organisation typically consists of hierarchically related series of organisation. As already mentioned, cognitive structures undergo progressive changes according to the principles of organisation determined by the function of the differentiation, isolation and rigidity.

Social factors in perception

Perception is a peculiar mental process influenced by a variety of feelings and emotions forming experience. In other words, the psychological factors of perception can hardly be brushed aside. In some experiments, it has been found that the accuracy of shape perception depends upon not only the shape but also the surrounding. For example, if some shapes are shown in a very dim light, they appear to be circular before the actual shape can be fully discriminated. Another experiment shows that there is a general tendency to perceive any shape with the maximum degree of simplicity, regularity and symmetry. The Gestalt psychology attached more importance to the forms of the object known as configuration. They also stressed the importance of meaningfulness in the field of perception. It appears that visual mechanism of the eyes and the brain do not readily offer a correct information of the stimulus present before our senses. Detail must be observed if they (complex shapes) are to be perceived. Greater intensity of illumination is required and at the same time more time is needed. As mentioned before, the surroundings have effect on perception. Judgment of shape tends to be subjective as the objects cannot be isolated from the context offering a scope for illusion. It also seems that normally we relate the size of any object to the sizes of all other objects in the total surrounding at that distance. The size is, therefore, perceived in relation to the size, and scale of the object and the distance. Thus there are factors like, shape, distance, illumination, context and previous experience which influence one's perception. These are more or less psychological because they have got a direct bearing on the conditioning of perception and the stimulus. On the other hand, there are factors which influence perception even without having any direct bearing on it. For example, motivation is related to perception. In other words, perception is affected by motives to a considerable extent. In one experiment observers were shown blurred pictures of articles related to food and of their household articles at varying periods after the last meal. There was an increase of value and brightness in the number of food-related objects perceived after about six hours after the last meal. But thereafter there are a decrease. In another experiment, the pictures of food and other objects are shown as first very dimly and then increasingly brightly. The brightness at which the food objects were perceived decreased up to about 3 to 4 hours after the observer's last meal and then increased again. It appeared, therefore, that there was at first, a tendency for food and related articles to be perceived more readily, but the observer became increasingly frustrated and ceased to take the trouble of responding as hunger increased. This again suggest that the observers become apathetic during their periods of deprivation. There are other experiments which show clearly that there is a complex interaction between need and expectation. The individual in a state of need is in a better position to perceive something which will satisfy his needs provided he can sure of the thing he wants, at the right moment. Another interesting observation justifies a positive correlation between the degree of aggressiveness and the speed of perception. From these experimental findings, it is obvious that perception is highly susceptible to the influence of various internal and external factors. The effect of values on perception has also been demonstrated by different experiments. A different type of interest and value effecting perception is related to people's relation to one another. This is a social factor that affects the manner in which they perceive those whom they like or dislike. Observers were asked to rate photographs of Negroes and Whites as to the degree they showed certain Negro characteristics. Those observers who were prejudiced against Negroes showed a definite tendency to exaggerate the degree to which these characteristics appeared in the Negro photographs.

There are various experiments which confirm this finding. Several other studies have been made·to prove that individuals judgement is influenced by of a group of the opinions expressed by other members of the group. Numerous experiments have been carried out to demonstrate the effect of various forms of valuation upon the perception of certain peculiar qualities of object.

The earliest experiment was one by Bruner and Goodman in which ten-year old children were required to adjust the size of a disc of a light to equal the sizes of coin and cardboard discs. It was found in general that they tended to overestimate the sizes of coins by comparison with the size of the cardboard disc. The more valuable the coins, the greater was the degree of overestimation.

Moreover, children from poor homes overestimated to a greater extent than did those from well-to-do homes. Unfortunately, the experiment repeated on various occasions has shown varying results. Other studies have been made to investigate on perception. Here also the results have been different and even contradictory.

Like other factors, success and failure, pleasure and pain are also influenced by perception. This has been shown by a number of experiments. In short, the complex process involved in perception is yet to be analysed. It has been clear that perception is influenced by various internal, and external factors no doubt, but the amount of interaction between these has not yet been explored. It is extremely difficult to isolate one variable from the other.

Gestalt Psychology and its Bearing on Perception

Research in the field of human behaviour has recently revealed a new world. The gradual dawn of psychological knowledge has flashed light on the mysteries of perception and thought processes. We still think of psychology as a young science growing and gradually extending its scope. Introspection as a psychological method has been accepted and there has been little scope for doubt about its importance. It is a fact that an attempt has been made to raise the status of psychology by considering it as a science of consciousness. As a result, functional psychology became more important that structural. While the former struggled for finding out the elements comprising mental life, the latter sought to discover the needs and expressions of inner organism. This new trend inspired Watson to discover the biological significance of the conscious processes and make an objective study by suitable means. A strong feeling of temptation to ignore the complexity of human mind expressed itself in the form of behaviourism.

The limitations of the behaviourism emerging in America did not escape the vigilance of a group of young psychologists in Germany. This group used the word "Gestalt" as its slogan and was known as the Gestalt school. The old idea of association was rejected and the new concept in terms of experience was brought to light.

Gestalt psychology emphasised the complex process of organisation of experiences. They tried to discover the relationship between the part and the whole in our perceptual fields. In other words, a pattern or form was recognised to play a part in the process of perception. There is no doubt that, the Gestalt psychologists have insisted most strongly on the organised wholeness of behaviour. The dynamics of brain activity presented another problem to the Gestalt school. It has been persistently held by the school that much of our experience which has been regarded as built upon sensation by higher mental process is really included in sensation. They urge that the sensory brain process is part and parcel of the total situation and also that the primary brain response does not depend simply on the visual stimulation, but also on other factors on total situations.

6

LEARNING AND ITS IMPLICATIONS

In the opinion of a school, any stimulation reaching the brain is taken up into a dynamic interacting system and its effects thereby depend on the total activity going on in the brain. In short, the Gestalt psychologists emphasised the total process controlling the brain response to the separate item of stimulation. Thus the influence of background and pattern has been pointed out and demonstrated by the Gestalt psychologists. The various demonstrations particularly in the visual field proved the limitation of our senses and the role of the inner brain dynamics in determining the shape or pattern emerging out of it.

From the day of Eblinghaus up to a subsequent date the psychological theory tended to build up a mechanical conception of learning. The Gestalt psychology tried to look at the field of learning and perception more closely, than others and stressed the importance of insight in learning. The instinctive responses indicated that trial and error behaviour have little value for effective learning which demands insight and direction. The organisation and reorganisation of experience in the light of changing circumstances is the key word used by the Gestalt psychologists. The perceptual factor in learning is emphasised by the school and true learning, according to this school, means doing something new to reach the goal. The gap is bridged up by meeting the situation.

The term insight, of courses, is relative because it may vary in respect of order and degree. Higher the order of insight, greater is the learning. As it stands today, the Gestalt school has still much possibility. The process of dynamic organisation in the field of perception has been analysed by the school, for further exploration into the perceptual process long neglected.

Nature and Scope of the Learning Process

Teaching has been defined as a process of continuous adjustment, leading to improvement of the behaviour of the learner. This adjustment takes place in course of learning which stimulates the experience and even the perception of the child. As the child learns, he gains more and more experience which helps him to understand the environment more closely than before. The relationships between the various factors in the environment are gradually discovered. With the enrichment of experience, an insight emerges and the situation proves more meaningful to the learner. Thus, a continuous development takes place in the learner's cognitive, affective and conative life.

Learning has been described mainly as a process, because it is a progressive function in human behaviour, a multipolar process. It involves the learner, the teacher as well as the environmental factors. It is a sort of process of interaction between the learner and the other factors around him. On the one·hand, the learner has his own needs, drives and propensities, while the environmental stimulation helps him to meet those needs in the learning situation.

While learning, one acquires some knowledge and experience and retains them for future guidance. Thus, learning involves both acquisition and retention. But all this acquisition and retention should have a reference to some goal. If there is a definite goal, learning becomes more effective as a result of motivation. Motivation is the essential condition for learning, and much depends upon how a learner can be motivated. It is a fact that, the need-satisfaction brings motivation in learning. The teacher is, therefore, required to know means of creating motivation in learning. Practice facilitates learning no doubt. But this is not all. There are certain types of learning which requires perceptual orientation and this is possible by means of effective stimulation of the learner's mental process. Their previous experience also helps better adjustment to new situation.

Learning involves a number of stages as every learning depends upon certain factors, internal and external. Among the internal factors, motivation and individual drives deserve mention. It is a fact that age and learning are also related, because maturation is a determining factor, for effective learning. It is a complex process involving acquisition and retention. At the same time, it is an active process.

It entails a journey from known to unknown beset with variety of experiences. Laboratory experiments have yielded valuable data on learning and forgetting. It has been found out that learning takes place in a rhythmic manner and, increase or decrease in learning may be due to several causes.

Learning curves have been introduced for graphic representations. Some phases of the progress made in successive attempts to learn a new skill, may be represented by Curves.

Curves vary from situation to situation. In some curves positive and negative acceleration takes place; while curves may also have plateaus, that is, periods when there is neither a rise nor a fall. The knowledge of the fluctuations in learning is helpful to a teacher. Learning curves of one individual for a short period of time are not so reliable as there may be rise and fall in the strength of motives or interest, or there may be other factors, like distractions or fatigue. Besides, learning curves help the learner to know his progress and the extent of progress of learning for better adjustment. Learning curves are also useful to the teachers for diagnostic purposes.

Some fundamental questions, still persist around learning. How permanent is learning, how much of what is learned or retained, and for how long, are some of the basic questions. Experiments have been conducted for objective finding. It has been found out that learning by itself, is not sufficient unless it is frequently assessed by active recalls. So, recall helps the learning process and frequent attempts of recall, reinforce learning. Recall requires more participation by the learner, than does reading or listening. It also ensures greater confidence in the learning. In addition to recall as a method of learning, recognition also plays a very prominent part. As a method, recognition stimulates learning although it is doubtful whether it is as effective as recall. There are various factors influencing learning. It is assumed that age is one of them and many believe that childhood is the best age for learning. But the findings of the experiments show that learning ability increases upto the age of 16 or 17. Learning ability varies not with age but with learning materials. Their value and the degree of interest they can arouse, are all important considerations. Motivation forms the pivotal factor in the dynamics of learning process. It is agreed that learning is much facilitated if the motivation and a need for learning are aroused. This brings an action and propels the learning to a considerable extent.

So far as the retention of learning is concerned, one has, no doubt, the need for preserving the experiences derived from learning.

Retention is also an individual capacity varying from person to person.

It is rather difficult to see how permanent will be learning in individual cases. Recall is a more active process which helps learning and also strengthens retention. During recall the learner gives much more attention than what he has done during learning. The confidence of the learner is also acquired during recall. As a method of testing what learning has been retained, recognition is also of much use. Through tests which demand recognition of the right response a learner reinforces his experience.

Educational Implications

The whole learning process is rather complex and one has to be careful at the time of application of this knowledge in the field of education. A teacher has to consider the individual differences in the capacity of learning and retention, while drawing up certain educational programme. At the same time the teacher must know how to create motivation among the students.

The methods of teaching, the use of the materials and aids of teaching and the interpersonal relationships between the teacher and the pupils are of much importance in the field of learning and teaching. As regards the method, it is obvious that the same technique doesn't apply universally, because much depends upon the materials to be learnt. In spite of the controversy on relative value of the whole and part methods, it has been found that the learning material should be studied as a unit although the difficult parts should be tackled separately. But this should not be regarded as a rule because a question of the learner's ability comes in. If the learner is less mature, the part method may be more useful. Thus, there is a scope for selection of methods according to the situation.

Learning is thus a process by which an activity is originated or changed. The characteristics of the change in activity cannot be explained on the basis of native response tendencies, or maturation of temporary states of the organism. The above operational definition of learning points out that learning is a deliberate process and not an instinctive activity or a product of certain maturation.

The time of maturation of behaviour sequence through regular stages is independent of intervening practice. A child does not learn to talk until it is old enough. The child behaves under the influence of maturation. Similarly, learning is different from reflex activities or instinctive behaviours which do not involve any cognitive process. It is thus difficult to formulate a comprehensive definition of learning because it is a complex process including a variety of activities. There are a few who believe that learning is related to problem solving and reasoning as well. Similarly, there are others who define learning as a change in the central nervous system, Learning takes place mysteriously and we can hardly know what happens inside the organism when learning occurs.

There are few typical problems around learning theories as follows:—

(a) What are the limits of learning ?

(b) What is the role of practice in learning?

(c) How important are drives and incentives, rewards and punishments ?

(d) What is the place of understanding and insight ?

(e) Does learning of one thing help to learn something else ?

There are the basic questions which very often confront a psychologist struggling for a full proof definition of learning. So far, learning theories have been classified under two major heads, viz. stimulus response theories and cognitive theories. In the former category the name of Thorndike, Skinner and Hull are specially mentioned, while in the later the names of Tolman, Lewin and other Gestalt psychologists deserve mention. The basis of learning has to be discovered before any further exploration will be attempted. It has been seen that Thorndike accepted as basis of learning the association between sense impressions and impulses to self expression. Such an association has also been known as a bond or connection which might be strengthened or weakened in the making and breaking of habits. Although Thorndike's theory has undergone remarkable modifications, the three postulates to explain the theories of learning are very fundamental. They are laws of readiness, exercise and effect.

The law of readiness states the circumstances under which a learner tends to be satisfied or annoyed. Readiness means preparation for action. Thus it is quite likely that interests and motives influence one's readiness to learn.

Another postulate of Thorndike, namely the law of exercise refers to the strengthening of the connections with practice and the weakening of connections or forgetting when practice is discontinued. The last but not the least important law formulated by Thorndike is the 'law of effect' which states: "when a modifiable connection is made and is accompanied by satisfying state of affairs, the strength of the connection is increased." If the connection is formed by an annoying state of affairs, its strength is decreased. Besides the above theories, one of the major developments of Thorndike's laws was the discovery of the spread of effect and belongingness. According to the principle of belongingness, the connection is more easily learnt if the response belongs to the connection it strengthens. Similarly, the discovery of the spread of effect has brought certain new concepts. It has shown that the influence of the rewarding state of affairs acts not only on the connection to which it belongs but also on adjacent connections both before and after the rewarded connection. The effect acts to strengthen, even punished, connections in the neighbourhood of the rewarded one. Thus it is interesting to note that the spread of effect is the most characteristic feature of most contemporary connectionism. Punishment has proved to be more effective. than Thorndike believed. It has been found by Stiffen that symbolic rewards strengthen weak connections more than symbolic punishment.

Estimate of Thorndike's Position

Thorndike's position on typical problems of learning may be summarized with reference to capacity, practice, motivation, understanding, transfer, forgetting etc. Learning capacity depends upon the number of bonds under the capacity. As regards practice, it has been seen that repetition of connection leads to an eligible strength unless the connections are rewarded. Practice is important because it permits rewards to act upon connection. Similarly, reward acts directly on neighbouring connection to strengthen them, while punishment has no corresponding direct weakening effect. The best way to get understanding is to build up a body of connections appropriate to the level of understanding. Reaction to the new situations benefits by the identity of the new situations in part with the old situation and principle of analogy described as assimilation.

7

REMEMBERING AND FORGETTING

Early theories of Remembering

The object of learning is really remembering. When we learn any thing, the ultimate object of our doing so is to retain what we have learnt.

The oldest theory of remembering like that of learning is association, and this idea was first given out by Plato. Plato said that we remember things by nearness or contiguity of experiences. Aristotle said that recall takes place through suggestions. One item causes us to recall another, because they are either similar or opposite in form. In both the cases there are certain significant points that suggest the second when the first is present.

David Hartley in the eighteenth century differentiated between two types of associations. If impressions are made simultaneously, we get synchronous association, otherwise we get successive association. In 1820, Brown put forward certain modification to Hartley's theory. He said that we associate and remember according to four conditions:

1. *Relative duration of the impression* : longer the duration the greater will be the impression received.
2. *Vividness :* the clearer the impression, the longer will it be remembered.
3. *Frequency :* the larger the number of impression, the greater will be the effect of them on the memory.
4. *Recency* : more recent events are better remembered than more remote ones.

Nine years later, James Mill repeated the same theory which had been started by Plato centuries earlier. It is the contiguity of associations that helps us to remember things. Hamilton, however, disputed this and held that one impression does not always revoke a single idea, but really recalls the whole situation of which both the impression and the association were parts. The sight of a lyre for instance, does not recall simply the tune or a particular player but the whole conference in which the tune was previously played, in which both the tune and the player will perhaps stands in prominence.

In 1885 Ebbinghause carried out his famous nonsense syllable experiments to analyse the function of learning and remembering. He thus attempted to reduce the problem to its basic elements. His experiments on learning and memory from a connected series deserve special mention. In remembering, much that is learnt is forgotten soon, but what remains is retained for a longer time and the rate of forgetting becomes slower as we proceed. The two factors involved in spacing learning periods for effective remembering are:

1. The length of the learning period, and
2. The successive interval between two learning periods.

Warden studying maze learning found that if a rat was forced to run in a maze in order to get its food, it learnt better successive practice for shorter periods for several days. But learning is not that effective when the practice was continued for one long period on a single day. There is, however, no hard and fast rule about the length of a period or the interval suitable for all cases. This will clearly depend on the nature of the task set. When the material is easy and the motivation is high, a longer period or two long periods of learning may do. But when the task is different or when the interest slackens it is possible that boredom will set in if the practice period is long. Weli distributed frequent short periods may be better.

Ebbinghause's Experiments on Learning and Memory

Though much criticised, the experiment on nonsense syllables by Ebbinghaus is a classical one being the first objective method to assess the relation of learning to retention. It also finds out to what extent do fatigue and boredom prevent both learning and retention. Ebbinghause selected nonsense syllables for examining the process of learning and remembering. He felt that when ordinary words are selected, they may convey different meanings for different individuals. Thus some persons have a better memory for certain words than others, and therefore, such words may be learnt better and remembered longer not for their basic qualities, but because they happen to have a greater stimulation. In selecting his syllable Ebbinghause, therefore, wanted them to be nonsense so that every learner may be placed at an equal disadvantage. He further made certain rules about their formation. The syllables should be so selected that the consecutive syllable should not together form a familiar word. Further all the syllables should be of the same length, if not, the longer or the shorter syllable may be remembered better because of its peculiarity. All syllables should be similarly constructed. He suggested that they should have two consonants and a vowel in between. The same vowel should not be repeated in two consecutive syllables nor should the initial and final consonants of two consecutive syllables be the same. Even the initial consonant of one syllable should not be same as the final consonant of its immediately proceeding syllable. All these, he held, would help in the retention of the pairs of syllables. All the syllables should be presented to the subject for exactly the same interval so that no one gets a prominence by a longer presentation. This can be ensured by presenting the syllables through a tachistoscope where the syllables are pasted on the roller and only one is visible through the opening. The movement of the roller is timed by a watch or a metronome. The number of trials or presentations necessary before a subject is able to recall, would demonstrate the rate of learning of a person. When the full list has been learnt, it has to be confirmed by a second presentation which should also be repeated in full. The number of words learnt on each presentation can be plotted on a graph and thus the learning curve may be drawn. This generally shows a steep rise at the start followed by a general flattening which is again followed by another steep rise. At the flat portion, evidently, learning has been slowed down and this Ebbinghause calls Plateau. There may be more than one plateau during learning in some cases. The existence of these plateaus signifies either fatigue or boredom.

Ebbinghause has also used his experiments to measure memory. This is measured by asking the subject to reproduce what he has learnt after an interval which may be from a few hours to a few days, Evidently, one does not remember the whole list fully and therefore needs another series of successive presentations before he can recall the whole list again. But it is also seen that in relearning he needs fewer presentations than before. The difference between the number of presentations on the first and on the second occasions would be an index of the person's memory. Presenting the list after successive intervals, sometime longer and sometimes shorter, may help us in finding out the rate of forgetting. Ebbinghause found that 44% of the original material in nonsense syllables are usually retained after an hour to two. After nine hours this falls to 30% and after two days it falls down to 28%. There is, however, a lot of individual differences. Some persons are found to remember the whole list even weeks after. In India it has been found, that on an average, the retention of nonsense syllables is higher. Over half is remembered after two hours, 37% after 8 hours and 31% after a week. The experiment thus serves several purposes. Subjectively, it can compare the memories of two persons. Objectively, it shows the important fact that much of what we learn is forgotten at the earlier stage.

Seashore repeated the experiment using nonsense geometrical figures where each figure consisted of three lines, two of equal length and one shorter (resembling Ebbinghause's distribution of vowels and consonants) so arranged that they neither resembled any letter or an alphabet known to the subject nor any known geometrical figure. With these results, we can likewise draw learning curve for the initial set of presentation and memory curve for successive presentations. He also got result like Ebbinghause regarding forgetting.

Psychologists like Bartlett have criticised the technique of Ebbinghause. They hold that when remembered the syllables no longer remain nonsense. The subject by virtue of some association, if no logical association is available, creates a certain amount of sense. Perhaps certain sounds in nonsense syllables and certain configuration of space in geometrical figures create stimuli of meaning. Thus all that Ebbinghause and others have done is to drive out the natural stimulus of meaning and create room for accidental and totally uncontrolled factors. The bonds of accidental associations, will naturally be different with different persons.

Researches after Ebbinghause

Researches after Ebbinghause have established that mere passage of time does not cause a person to forget. Other factors like interest and tension come in for they cause better attention. Zeigarnik gave a number of pupils some twenty puzzles to solve and along with these puzzles he included a few problems which touched matters of their interest.

While the pupils were working for the first half of the period the pupils were interrupted, but for the other half they were free from interruptions. Normally one should expect that the second half which proceeded without interruption would be remembered better, and that they would forget most of what they had learnt during interruption. But contrary to expectations, it was found that they remembered and could recall more of the solutions that had been performed in the midst of interruption, than those which proceeded without interruptions. Zeigarnik explains this strange behaviour by asserting that since interruptions created a tension in the mind, attention was evoked better by the tension and hence the subjects could remember better.

Emotion affects both learning and memory. Freud explains forgetting in terms of his theory of repression. We tend to forget unpleasant memories and ideas because we repress them. In the same way we forget the names or faces of persons we dislike. Meltzer and Stagner have however tried to work out quantitatively the extent to which dislike aids in helping us to forget. It seems from their experiments that the amount is not very large, being only the 15%. Evidently, both Freud and the other experimenters show that when repression causes a certain amount of tension, forgetting would not be so easy.

Jenkins and Dallenbach have shown that if after learning a new thing, we fall asleep, we are likely to remember it better than when we keep awake after learning. The explanation of this is obvious. When we are awake we can not help new impressions entering into our minds and these would certainly overlap and reduce the intensity of the impressions. But when we fall asleep immediately, we prevent such possibility and this helps us to retain things.

Muller and Pilzckar have found that memory of a newly learnt poem may be interfered due to learning a second poem. Subjects were found to recall 56% or even more of the learnt material, if there had been no additional assignments imposed. But when engaged in more than one task, they can recall less than half, often 26% or less. This is also due to other impressions overlapping. Busy people are often found absent minded, because new images are being blurred by the appearance of overlapping images. This they called 'Retroactive Inhibition.'

Jost has found a principle of review which is commonly known as Jost law. Stated briefly, it holds that if two associations are of equal strength, but have been formed at different periods, it will be seen that with passage of time the older one will lose its intensity though rather slowly. In order to retain a learnt material, therefore; frequent relearning and review are essential. Thus, Jost really found the same for memory what Thorndike had stated for learning by two laws of Frequency and Recency.

A mysterious effect was noticed by Ballard in 1913. He found that sometimes after the passage of time, old and forgotten things become vivid once more, even if an attempt of review is not made. This he calls "Reminiscence" and should not be taken as opposing Jost law in any way. Ballard's findings are for single items that are learnt, while Jost's findings relate to a comparative retention of two items. Ballard's findings are also complementary to Ebbinghause's findings, for he assumes that after an initial learning, a lot of learned material seems to be forgotten. What Ebbinghause assumed as forgotten, Ballard holds that they merely sink to the bottom of the mind so to speak. Some of these sunk materials may suddenly rise up under certain conditions. Strictly speaking, reminiscences are not so well found in case of nonsense materials. It has generally to do with experiences which are more meaningful. Perhaps by getting fresh stimulus of association, conscious or unconscious, there is a sort of perception and therefore, the old things also come up. This kind of reminiscence is more common with childhood experience than with experiences of later times.

Remembering in terms of Gestalt Theory

Gestalt theory holds that all mental phenomena have a structure or pattern, and that ideas and events are never isolated. They always exist with some connection or association with each other. If these connections are just perceived or vaguely remembered, naturally they will not have so much effect as when they are intelligently perceived. When relations are duly understood, Gestalt theory proves why it is easier to remember the whole poem rather than stanza. Gestalt theory will explain "Retroactive Inhibition" or interference of one learnt material by another. It assumes that either they do not represent two different portions of the same pattern or two contrasting patterns, or else if they belong to the same pattern or configuration, they interfere because connections between them are not well understood. Reminiscence according to Gestalt is nothing but a rehearsal of the entire situation which comes up when the general pattern is recalled and all the portions including things that were apparently forgotten get recalled.

Summary

The gains of learning are really in the direction of retention and remembering. As in learning so in remembering, the associationists offer the explanation that by creating bonds of association experiences are retained and so are the bundles of thought. Hartley and Mill as well as Brown subscribed to this theory and made substantial personal contributions to it. The best and the most well known experiment on Association had been those by Ebbinghause in nonsense syllables. The conditions imposed on the selection of syllables and on their presentation prevented any type of bias from creeping in and the experiment was able to show the nature of learning and of forgetting. Learning and memory curves showed for instance, plateaus of boredom or fatigue during learning. The results indicated that much is forgotten at the initial stage. His experimental results have been corroborated by similar experiments in other fields, notably by Seashore. Psychologists like Bartlett, however, express some doubt whether Ebbinghause has after all succeeded in driving out the stimulus of meaning. They hold that perhaps accidental associations are able to give meanings to these nonsense syllables.

Recent researches like those of Freud, Meltar and Stagner have proved that our retention is not merely dependent on the article, but more on the attitude of the learner. The common assumption is that interruption causes distractions and makes us forget things quickly. But that is not the real fact. They may cause tensions and thereby things get better remembered causing the mind to strain calling forth better attention. Emotional changes and interest are also vital factors. When two things are learnt simultaneously one learning overlaps with the other. This perhaps explains Jenkin's findings why we seem to remember better when we fall asleep immediately after learning. Muiler and Flizkar have given a special name to this interference of the second material namely Retroactive inhibition. Of the two associations the older one is forgotten unless reviewed. This is really a repetition of Thorndike's Laws of Frequency and Recency. Ballard found that very often forgotten things are brought back into the mind, proving that they remained sunk perhaps at a subconscious mind, proving that they remained perhaps at a subconscious level.

8

ATTENTION AND INTEREST

What is attention

Attention is the name of that condition within a person which enables him to be clearly aware of a certain object or activity. It is a condition of preparedness or alertness.

While sensation means merely receiving certain stimuli of which we are just conscious of, perception means the general awareness of these stimuli. In perception, therefore, the sensations which are received convey some meaning. Attention is focussing perception in a definite direction. In a way therefore, attention is a cause and an aspect of perception. In order that perception may acquire some meaning, it is necessary that certain features of perception have to be focussed. Yet it must not be supposed that we attend to only one thing at a time. About a hundred years ago Sir William Hamilton noted that as many as six or seven different objects can be perceived at a time. Cattell found that adults can apprehend six to eleven objects at a time, and if the items occur in meaningful groups many more can be comprehended. Thus if letters are grouped into words and the latter into meaningful short sentences, as many as thirty can be comprehended at a time. It is thus found that in such a situation, the sentence is comprehended as one single unit. Attention may also be described as a process of adjustment of the organism to the stimulus situation.

William Jones has divided attention into kinds, in various ways. It is either sensorial attention or objects connected with sense or intellectual attention, where the objects are represented either by ideas or written symbols.

Thus when we concentrate on a toy or a picture, the attention is sensorial. When we are reading a book, the meaningful words are expressed by mere symbols and hence the attention is intellectual.

When the book represents a story with complex characterisation, the intellectual element is still further raised to a higher level. In another system of classification, attention may be immediate, when the topic or stimulus is interesting by itself without relation to ànything else. Thus as the sweets are presented to the child, the child pays attention to the movement and the attention is immediate. But attention may also be derived in which case the child's immediate interest may not be connected with the thing acting as the stimulus, but the source of interest springs from an object with which the particular stimulus is associated. Thus a student may pay attention to a verse not because the verse itself is interesting, but because the student has been promised a reward on successful recitation of the verse. The source of interest here lies in the promised reward. In the successful learning the attention may either be passive, involuntary and effortless or active and voluntary: Involuntary attention always accompanies an intense or voluminous or sudden impulse. It is always immediate and generally sensorial, though rarely intellectual. When we are posing to take photograph the sudden flare of the flash light may draw our immediate attention. While in a running bus, the sight of a magnificent building may likewise draw our attention and so would unexpected appearance of a person who has been reported as dead. But all our sources of attention are not involuntary. Some times we make an effort at attending to some thing. Voluntary attention is always for a derived object. If the stimulus is interesting by itself, attention will come spontaneously and involuntarily. But if it is not so, we consciously make associations of the source of our attention. The particular stimulus which is before us, directs our effort to the latter in order to reach the former. Though generally intellectual, voluntary attention may be sometimes directed to sensorial subjects as well.

Constancy of Attention

James has also found that the nature of stimuli for attention fluctuates with age. While children are more excited with immediately exciting and sensorial stimuli, the adults are generally trained to select those stimuli which are connected with permanent interests. It is, therefore, no wonder that the famous mathematician Archemedes could quietly work out mathematical problems amidst the din and noise of the Roman invasion. He was so engrossed in his work that he took no precaution to save his life and ultimately met a tragic death.

Cruze says that the teacher who requests 'whole and undivided' attention of the members of his class is guilty of a loose talk. Attention can not but be whole and undivided for the moment when one concentrates towards a particular stimuli. The stimulus may be a picture or a group of words, a statue which we see, or a musical note we hear, or an object with fragrance. It is of course possible that attention may fluctuate or the focus may move from one stimulus to another. The continual shifting of attention should not, however, worry a teacher unless the shifting takes place outside the general area. The person reading an exciting novel shifts his attention from line to line, from page to page and yet his attention to the novel is sustained for hours. The spectators of a match shift their attention from one side of the play ground to another along with the running ball and yet their attention to the game remains sustained till the match is over. The best way to maintain a sustained attention is thus by developing an intense interest in that area or activity. When other stimuli begin to draw attention from the object to which we want to focus our attention, we call the latter distractors. When we are distracted, we are attending to the situation, which we feel should not be receiving our attention. Distraction, like attention may be sensorial, viz. noise, want of light, bad smell or any attractive object, or it may be intellectual. It may either be immediate or derived. It may be external or internal. Hunger, nausea, tension, worry, anxiety and similar things act as internal distrauctors. Distractions are thus conflicts between stimuli and we try to avoid them. Thus we may avoid distraction of the noise in the hostel and go to study in a quiet park. We may also overcome distractions by spending an increased amount of energy.

Determinants of attention are the factors that produce the condition of attention in a person. They may be internal or external. The nature, size, duration and intensity of the stimulus comprise external determinants. The internal or subjective determinants are interest, needs, desires and purposes of the individual.

Interest : its importance

People vary greatly in their interest, which acts as the source of motivating attention. The same situation may produce different kinds of interest to different persons. Thus a farmer inspecting a plot of land would be interested in the nature of the soil and plants growing on it, while a geologist will be more attracted in the layers of rocks exposed. A contractor may look at the same plot and think of how it can be subdivided and used to make residential buildings, while an artist would walk round until he found the position from which the landscape looked as a balanced composition would be painted. Thus all the four persons are looking at the plot with different interests and each is focussing his attention from a particular angle and point of interest. The interests supply the necessary source of energy to focus attention or to sustain it and also to overcome distractions, if any. Thus it is found that we may spend the same time in reading a novel as we might in working a number of mathematical sums. Yet we shall probably feel a greater strain in the latter. It is because the latter act is of less interest. It has been seen that interest reduces the fatigue considerably and the work itself proceeds quite smoothly. What will constitute an interest? Are we interested in an act whose outcome brings us to a desirable end? This leads to a further question, who is to decide and what end is desirable? The answer to that is, it is the pupil who has ultimately to decide. A real interest can not be created, it has to be generated within the person. Interests are not totally inborn, they are acquired in course of interaction with the society in which we live. In most of the cultures men are more interested in adventure, in physical activity, in mechanics, in aggressive games, while the women are mostly interested in artistic work, in domestic activities and in social services. It is so because these are the roles that men and women play respectively in their later lives in cultures. Alexander Goldenwiser has found that in some of the cultures hunting is done by women and cooking and housekeeping by men.

It is thus clear that, if we want the child to be interested in any educational activity, we must generate interests in particular areas. In other words, education will be interesting, if it is connected with life.

How to make our lessons interesting

In order to make the lesson interesting, we must connect it with real life situations. Dewey has further stated that in order to sustain interest, the goal should be quite visible. Analysing the play activities, he states that the reason why a child is interested in the play activities is that, the outcome of the play is immediate. The child's action immediately leads to a result. In our so-called activities, the child is not so interested simply because the outcome is so far off. How can we expect a child to put in strenuous effort at the beginning of the session in his class work, if the outcome of his efforts will produce results at the end of the whole year? He thus advises us to devise our programme in such a general way that we may say that interests are created in socially useful activities. One may probe deeper and find out the particular region in which an individual is interested. For these we have individual interest tests. Most interests are measured by personal inventories. The subject indicates his likes and dislikes by appropriate markings of words and phrases, measures of interest, tests of information of objects and activities. There are special interest inventories and tests like Strong's Vocational Interest Blank. 400 items comprise the Blank and the subject marks them with his remarks 'like' indifferent' or `dislike'. Thrustone, analysing the Blank found that there are really four basic interests: Science, Language, people and business. Similar interest tests are available for recreational, literary and other fields of activities.

Summary

Attention is focussing perception in a definite direction. Though a person can direct his attention to several things almost simultaneously, it has been found that he really focuses his attention either to one single object or to a cluster of objects. Attention can be divided in various ways, it may be sensorial or directed to object of immediate perception. It may be intellectual or directed to objects represented by ideas or symbols. It may be immediate. Or it may be derived in which the thing may merely act as a stimulus to an outside object or idea. Attention may also be passive, involuntary or active. It has been seen that while immediate, interests are always involuntary, derived ones are voluntary or active. The latter distinction does in no way differentiate between sensorial or intellectual attention. Both of these can either be passive or active though in a majority of cases intellectual attention is active. While children are more excited with immediately exciting and sensorial stimuli, more mature persons are generally trained to select matters of more remote and permanent interest. Attention is seldom steady as it fluctuates. There is no harm if this fluctuation is kept within bounds. Any one reading an interesting novel shifts his attention from line to line, and yet retains his major interest in the outcome of the story he follows. Distractors like noise, bad illumination, act as impediments to attention. These may be immediate or derived, external as well as internal like hunger, worry or anxiety.

Relationship between attention and interest

Attention is closely related to interest as interest brings motivation. It is essentially a matter of enduring settings of our conative tendencies and impulses and is determined by our instincts and sentiments. Dewey affirms that genuine interest is the accompaniment of the identifications, through action, of the self with some object or ideas. According to Vernon, "an interest is just as complex as an amalgam of subjective feelings and objective behaviour tendencies." These feelings and tendencies propel human drives and reinforce attention.

INTEREST—ITS BEARING ON MEMORY AND ATTENTION

Interest is a word with different shades of meaning. Drever describes interest as both functional and structural.

The feeling of worthwhileness accompanying attention to an object or activity, may be ascribed to the functional sense of the term, while element in make up is structural. Although it is usual to regard interests as personality traits, together with attitudes, needs and aptitudes, the structure of personality has not yet secured agreement on its basic dimensions. While some progress has been made recently, the study of Interests awaits exploration.

The difficulty should not be under rated. As mentioned before, there are various aspects of interest involving the cognitive process, affective and the conative elements. On the other hand, there are other aspects which may be roughly described as dimensions.

Dimensions of Interest

Very few have doubted the complexity of interest. The expressions of interest are too diverse to be detected. In the first place, intensity may be termed as one of the dimensions. This dimension in question may include psychological energy or dynamic power with which the interest is charged. Nature of interest may be taken as another dimension of interest.

Duration of interest may be assumed to be the third dimension of interest. Nature of interest may be indicated by the type of organisation within the mind. Interest may thus be potential or acquired.

Memory traces of past experience conditioned by inherited propensities and by the physical and social environment may give some indication of the nature of interest.

The cognitive aspect of an interest is first noticeable involving attention, perception, discrimination and judgment. The selectivity of attention that accompanies interest is remarkable. It also involves the dispositions to attend to a particular object to select, discriminate and compare. It refers to the organisation of past experiences and to the immediate recall of selected elements to meet the interest situation.

The weighing of certain elements in the schemata might be determined by the senses or by drives, but with adults mostly through the operation of persistent interests.

It has also been recognised that in any interest situation there is present an affective element, that is, a feeling or emotion. This is implied in such terms as "self-identification" and "ego-involvement". In the "dynamic" psychology of recent years, this feeling is related to the state of tension existing in the subject's mind.

The feeling is accompanied by a discharge of psychological energy which has accumulated on the interest.

The conative element of striving towards a goal appears to be distinctive. It is, however, possible that there would exist certain relationships between the aspects or dimensions of interest. For example, the intensity of interest may be more related to the affective aspects. But the more perturbing question is to determine the nature of interest and discriminate between what is potential and acquired.

Emphasis is also being laid on the determinants of behaviour. According to Allport, personality represents an individual's style and mastery within his behavioural field.

In order to test the hypothesis that there exists a good deal of overlapping between various aspects and dimensions of interest one has to construct suitable instruments designed to measure each aspect and dimension already formulated. Centroid analysis of the inter-correlations may reveal the fact whether there are so many aspects or dimensions.

If various dimensions emerge out of factor analysis it would be evident that the existing approaches to the assessment of interest and other personality variable are far from being adequate.

The history of measurement of interest shows that both subjective and objective approaches have been made to assess interest in one or two dimensions. As a result, the earlier attempts have not been crowned with full success. Among the earlier classifications, most of the attempts are towards taking up one of the dimensions of interest and approaching the problem by means of one or two techniques. Inventory has been employed mainly for attacking the cognitive aspect of interests whereas information tests and other techniques have been employed for attacking the unconscious level of interest formation.

In the broadest terms there has been a constant shift of emphasis from one sense of the term to the other. It is a fact that the complexity of the nature of interest has been brought to the notice and considered while constructing the test.

The study of the structure of personality has not yet secured agreement on its basic dimensions, and so the approaches to the assessment have varied considerably. Another outstanding problem around interest is that of classification. Workers in this field were not particularly aware of this problem and they went on classifying interests in their own ways. This classification was really arbitrary and it is difficult to arrive at an agreed list of interests. If interests are interpreted as expressions of satisfaction of certain needs in the course of adjustment to environment, then it is likely that various kinds of interests would appear in various fields. On an analysis, however, it will be observed that interests are related to the various fields of activities as motivational factors. There have been attempts to find out the broad patterns of interests which can be roughly described as:-

1. Theoretical or intellectual.
2. Aesthetic or artistic.
3. Economic or utilitarian.
4. Mechanical or technical.
5. Scientific.
6. Social or humanitarian.
7. Religious or spiritual.
8. Political.

It is just obvious that these categories of interest may be superficial and the surface study of these might lead to nothing. According to Cattell, the reason behind the failure in a perfect classification may be attributed to the inability in constructing indirect measures of interests and attitudes. He also points out that the chief trend is in classifying general interests either under arbitrary, convenient logical categories or else by using factorial analysis and similar methods to find the groups in which interests cluster. It is, therefore, desirable that attempts should first be made to discover the basic patterns of interests.

Most of the classifications have been of a—priori nature and on the whole there is a tendency to use the five categories which may be called the "classical" ones.

(1) Aesthetic (2) Scientific (3) Social (4) Mechanical and (5) Business.

The writer was conscious of the difficulty of reconciling some of the results of previous study and an investigation was made to explore the field for improving the position. It has been found from a factorial study, carried out by the writer elsewhere that very few patterns of interests emerge out of factor analysis. The reasons were not far to seek. It was felt that the limited number of assumed variables may be one of the reasons for smaller numbers of factors emerging out of the analysis. He was not, therefore, convinced that the number of the basic patterns of interests is so limited.

9

MEANINGS, IMAGERY AND IMAGINATION

Importance of Meaning

Unfortunately much of what passes for learning in the classroom is really mechanically memorized statements which pupils cram without understanding. The inevitable dependence of learning upon meaning is thus being ignored. The language in which statements are given are really means of conveying thought and are the vehicles of ideas. They must, therefore, be understood, and not merely mechanically memorized. Confusion arises when words that are used are in areas remote from the perception or experience of the persons. Words, as such are used to symbolize experiences. Their capacity for conveying ideas depends not only on the extent they are able to convey experience. Meanings that these words stand for, are to be evolved out of perception. The perception of the child becomes more refined and generalized, as he becomes more and more aware of the detailed aspects of objects. Thus he recognized the difference between a round ball which has depth, and a round disc which is flat. Perception depends on the use and experience of an object. Dewey has given a good example of the circumstances under which the child learns the meaning of the word 'hat'. Probably his mother before taking the child out puts hat on the child's head. The child's primary interest lay in going out, for it meant seeing new things and going to new surroundings. But he at the same time noticed the inevitable connection between the putting on of the hat and going out. Thus the thing, hat, acquired a meaning for him because it was necessary to fulfil his interest. The child's interest in the hat was thus aroused and the hat became meaningful. Now, if the mother utters the word 'Hat' the child will notice the inevitable connection between the thing in which he was interested and the name. The word 'hat' now stands for the thing, and hence it becomes meaningful to the child. But if we ask a child the definition of 'hat', he will simply say, it is something to put on the head. Most of the children's definitions are similarly functional. A chair is something to sit on, a ball is something to kick. Perhaps these definitions may not seem to be quite logical or exhaustive but by this method of identifying objects by naming them without any mention of their specific characters, a child gets the primary basis of meanings. With experience, meanings are extended to other functions, than what the objects are supposed to stand for. This is more true when meanings are extended to actions besides objects. There is of course some connection between the fundamental or primary meanings and the secondary or derived meanings. The latter is more symbolic and convey something more than what is immediately perceived. But as words are used to convey certain experiences, a word becomes capable of conveying a primary and one or more derived meanings. It may give room for misunderstanding, for the experiences of the user and the listener may differ. As an example let us take the simple word 'lift' which is a word conveying an action namely 'to pick up'. This is the primary meaning of the word which everybody understands. But this word is capable of giving atleast four different types of meanings under four different situations:

1. Let us lift the book up from the shelf (Primary).
2. Give me a lift in your car from here to the Station.
3. He got a lift as he became the headmaster.
4. There is a lift, here in this building.

Misunderstandings are bound to crop up when the user speaks of the lift in one sense and the listener understandings in another. A village boy who has never seen a lift may feel that it literally picks up people or one who is not accustomed to giving or getting lifts in a car may feel that the driver literally picks up passengers and the like. Again one may think of a lift as a rise in the salary, while another may understand it as being given work at a place which is served by electric lifts.

From these derived meanings abstract concepts of a more generalised nature are developed. Of course not all the words are capable of this type of generalised meanings. But in those that are thus capable, there is perhaps a greater danger of misunderstanding. The user may utter a generalized word without realising its full implications. Such danger was responsible for the development of socratic method of counteracting the abstract definitions of the sophists. Such dangers are no less, evident today. Perhaps our restricted field of experience vitiates the meanings which these terms have in a wider context. But this word is capable of giving at least four different types of meanings under four different situations mentioned earlier.

1. Let us lift the book up from the shelf (Primary).
2. Give me a lift in your car from here to the Station.
3. He got a lift as he became the headmaster.
4. There is a lift, here in this building.

Misunderstandings are bound to crop up when the user speaks of the lift in one sense and the listener understands in another. A village boy who has never seen a lift may feel that it literally picks up people or one who is not accustomed to giving or getting lifts in a car may feel that the driver literally picks up passengers and the like. Again one may think of a lift as a rise in the salary, while another may understand it as being given work at a place which is served by electric lifts.

From these derived meanings abstract concepts of a more generalised nature are developed. Of course not all the words are capable of this type of generalised meanings. But in cases where one word has many meanings there is perhaps a greater danger of misunderstanding. The user may utter generalized word without realising its full implications. Such dangers are no less, evident today. Perhaps our restricted field of experience vitiates the meanings which these terms have in a wider context. To a labourer, Democracy perhaps means the rule of the mob on a strike day and social justice may convey the idea of an unruly meeting demanding a rise in wages. Their thoughtless use may produce such situations as may be embarrassing or dangerous. It is only after widening the field of experience so as to give a suitable opportunity for such generalisations that one should use them. Herein comes the role of the school. Since these abstract words are to be used in real life situations, it is the function of the school to provide an opportunity for imitating the life situations and to show the context in which such generalisations and abstract terms can be used. This is possible only when the school is connected with the life.

How can the meanings be clarified or enriched

One of the first steps that must be taken to clarify meanings should be to make the fullest use of the environment. Pupil's experience should be supplemented with a great variety of all types of visual aids available. These must as far as possible be the accurate representation of the reality. A toy motor should look like a real motor for instance, otherwise, they may convey hazy and incorrect impressions. In using these representations however, one should remember that aids are just aids and should not be confused with ends. They should not for instance be used in preference to real things when there are opportunities available for showing real things.

Since it is not always easy to communicate specific objects of experiences, as they are so many, we must classify such experiences and arrange them into groups so that they become more handy, useful and therefore, more meaningful. Here we are really borrowing the technique of the labour-saving device shown by associationists.

After generation, ideas have to be abstracted or the essential process must be taken out of the specific and concrete situations. This is possible by a careful survey of the specific or concrete situations and by extracting from them the essential element. The boy's idea of 'affection' for instance, is the result of the generalised concept of a number of concrete and specific situations of a mother fondling her child, a bird feeding its young, or a girl playing with her dolls. His concept of 'democracy' may likewise be built for him in the school by what he sees in orderly organisation of his literary societies, students' governments in his hostel or in the sports organisations.

We thus find that whatever be the type of the meaning, primary or secondary, generalised or abstract, we can get them only against the background of a concrete reality or specific cases and situations which clarify and enrich these meanings. Some of these concrete situations are of course provided by the home or other agencies that are giving informal education. It is the work of the school or any other institution where a teacher is to give a formal education to think of other situations and provide opportunities to the students to get as near as the concrete reality as possible. This, the schools can do provided they identify themselves with as many of the life situations as are practically possible for them to do.

Imagery and meaning

The meaning that is gained in any situation is stored in the mind in the form of images. These images are later recalled when the need for them arises. Images arise out of specific experiences, that an individual has. If a boy uses lift in the sense of a rise in the salary that his father might have got in the office, and another uses it in the sense of a free ride that a kind motorist gave him on a rainy day, it is because their experiences differ. Even abstract ideas are generalised experiences of a number of concrete situations.

We must, however, remember that the images are not merely conservative. They do not only retain whatever impressions are given, but sometimes they blend one or more images together and reconstruct something new, something that did not exist before. In such cases the images are the causes of imagination. One must have a stock of images gathered from the concrete reality as well as experience and a number of images built before they can be blended together.

Whether specific or, generalised, concrete or abstract, images help the children to form imagination.

A child of four or five by dramatising the situation, by playing the role of an engine driver, gets an opportunity for his diversion. He is really building up his images of the engine which he has once seen. Perhaps he is at the same time using the law of practice and repeats the process to get the images of the essential and perhaps symbolic forms of the functions of a railway engine. Perhaps this gives a clue to the schools about the methods they should follow in building up these images. They may likewise try to give opportunity to practice, with lifelike models or by dramatisation when real things are not available. This helps the learner to gain more impressions and to consolidate these in order that proper images may be formed.

Theories of Imagery

In the eighteenth and in early nineteenth centuries, psychologists used the term 'Image' in the same sense as they used 'Ideas', 'Associations', or 'Thought'. They assumed that memory and thinking involved a definite imagery.

Hume distinguished between impressions and images for the first time stating that whole impressions occur in presence of the objects; images are just faint copies of the original impressions. His views were shared by James Mill. Hartley tried to define images on a psychological basis.

He held that sensations cause nervous vibration and arouse miniature feeble vibrations within the brain. He believed that these vibrations build up images.

In 1860 Galton reported the astonishing results of his study on mental images by means of questionnaire which he had put to many persons. An ordinary man had after all a limited field of experience in which his images are formed. But wherever these images are formed they appear to be quite clear and well defined. In case of highly qualified and experienced scientist and literary men however, the case appeared to be quite reverse. They had no doubt images extended over many fields, but such images appeared to be quite blurred and diffused. Women and young boys had fewer but on the whole better defined images than men. Evidently, it seems there is something wrong with image formation in an educational surrounding. Galton ascribed the deficiency of imagery in the scientists to be due to the fact that they were called upon to do a lot of abstract thinking without a concrete background.

As the images are formed out of impressions, and the gateway for these impressions are the senses, it is necessary for us to find which sense in particular is more active in giving us the impression. Different persons it was found, used different senses. Perhaps, if we could ascertain which sense is predominating in which person, we may build up his imagery accordingly.

Kraplin and later Smith by using words and phrases conveying sense impressions with different sense areas have attempted to find out which sense department is more predominating. 'A cup' for instance gives the impression of a beautiful utensil to one and thus provides an opportunity to form a visual image To another with a more developed sense of smell or taste it may convey the flavour of delicious tea, a third with a specially developed taste for food, will probably smack his lips for some delicacy that can be served in the cup.

Kraplin used a number of phrases, from each of the five sense departments: visual (sight), gustatory (taste), olfactory (smell), tacticle (touch) and auditory (hearing). To these he added a sixth sense

Kinesthetic that implies motion. Kraplin's division of the original words or stimuli were such that they were equally divided. The classification of course being subjective, depends on the judgement of the experimenter. The subjects were asked to state the impressions, which these words seemed to convey. It was found that the experimenter's classification of the words convey the classification of the images the person experimented upon. Very often he gave more images in one or more sense departments and fewer impressions in others. Care should, however, be taken while performing this experiment that the actual objects are not present before the subject, for in that case it will be as case of perception rather than image formation. Smith repeated the experiment with phrases instead of words and found similar results. The educational implications of such experiments are important.

This can help to diagnose which happens to be more effective for the formation of impression of a particular student. This is the proper area in which he is apt to form his images, to suit his individual needs. We must so organise his impressions mostly through his more effective gateway of predominating sense perception. It is only then that his images will be meaningful.

Galton found that imagery of abstract things is some time peculiar. To some, different arithmetical numbers represent bars or lines of different lengths, while to others, these represent different colours and different shades of red, black or green. The images of different colours are some times blended with auditory tunes. When they see a red colour they are reminded of a peculiar tune and when they see a green colour they are reminded of another tune. Some people have hearing associated with colours. When they hear a particular tune they are reminded of one colour and for a different tune they have another colour. Such impressions are perhaps results of accidental or chance associations. They may often cause much embarrassment to the persons. The remedy lies in freeing them of these impressions quite early in their lines by producing the right type of impressions. They should have these abstract generalised concepts from many concrete impressions.

Stern tried to devise an objective measure of the amount and quality of imagery. He wanted to test how vivid an image a person can form, since all persons do not form equally vivid images. Stern would show a picture to a subject and ask him to recall as many details as he could possible do. In 1907, Urbantschits and later Jarnesch found that some persons have the remarkable capacity of recalling clear-cut images of things presented before them for a short time, say, half a minute. It is evident that the time is insufficient for a normal person to perceive so many details. Such persons are said to have idiotic Imagery. Often they would recall such details as might have escaped their conscious perception, thus proving that their perception has been at least, in part, somewhat subconscious. Allport however, finds nothing very wonderful in this idiotic imagery. It is the ordinary power of image formation only a bit quicker and morevivid.

Imagination

To a man in the street there is perhaps hardly any difference between mental imagery and imagination. Perhaps one may confuse imagination with mere day dreaming which represents an element of wishful thinking in which not only adolescents but some time adult as well as children indulge. While there is often an element of fantasy in day dreaming, or in imagination, as defined by psychologists, there is also a creative thinking.

It is a process that leads to practical and constructive ends, though it may not always lead to tangible results.

Helmhotz studies his own creative thought process. He found that they were results of prolonged deliberate effort which often made him tired and distracted. Solution would come to him in the form of inspiration after some time.

Rosman found that creative ideas would come to an inventor only when he is somewhat in a relaxed mood. It would come when a person is asleep and sometime after he would wake up after a sound sleep. Rarely however, they appeared just before dropping off to sleep. As one can sleep only when he is free from distractions and worry, it follows that creative thoughts can never come to a worried and perplexed mind, but would appear only when mind has got over the state of perplexity, conflict or confusion.

Ribot and later Graham Walls studies the process more scientifically and through their investigations showed some difference in minor points, although in essential points they both agreed. They found four essential elements in imagination :

1. First of all there must be a desire to solve the problem. This Graham calls the preparation state.
2. For a long time this desire troubles the person without bringing out any solution. It is a long and painful period of racking one's brain. Graham calls this the period of incubation in which ideas often recur in the mind, but does not give any solution to the problem.
3. This is followed up by a period of illumination or inspiration in which the solution appears as a flash. Often the person is surprised as to how he overlooked this simple solution so long. He realises that the painful brain-racking process of the incubation period has really brought the solution in a subconscious form, and this has now suddenly risen up to the conscious level with a rapidity that surprises the person himself.
4. Lastly, comes the period of verification or revision, where the validity or correctness of the inspiration is tested by application.

Creative imagination may easily be confused with day dreaming, and one must not overlook that abstract thinking is the cause of both. The fact that some of the great inventors and discoverers had been mere dreamers in their childhood or adolescence would go to prove that one begets the other. We have already shown why an individual tired or distracted in the real world, covers up his inadequacies by building an unreal world of his own. This often happens during adolescence, when the causes of this frustration are perhaps greatest.

If left to itself this leads not only to a wastage of time but produces a ban and withdrawing habit providing a refuge which an individual would resort to whenever he feels frustrated in real life. Yet if properly directed, it may give the individual an opportunity to work out great things. Creative thinking is not the monopoly of a favoured or fortunate few. It is open to all who have a good stock of concrete images which are to blend and fuse together and to all who are ready to take sufficient pains.

Summary

Though commonly confused, rote or mechanical memory is not the same as meaningful learning or images. Because words are symbolised forms of experiences, there is a danger that the sense conveyed by the person communicating may not be understood by the person receiving information. If meaning is derived by the use of concrete objects, the chances of such misunderstandings are considerably reduced. Sometime, however, from the primary meaning an expression has many secondary or derived meanings, each of which becomes clear to a person who has had the experience of the thing, or situations in which such derived meanings have originated. From the derived meanings come the generalised or abstract meanings.

To enrich or clarify pupil's store of meanings, teachers should first of all make fullest use of the environment. Experiences are often classified into groups so that similar images may be formed.

Before abstraction, a careful survey of several concrete situations out of which such abstract situations have generated must be made. Whatever be the type of meanings, primary (concrete) or secondary, generalised or abstract, we must have a rich background of the concrete reality or specific cases and situations which make such meanings clear and remove chances for misunderstanding.

Meaning that is gained out of a concrete situation is stored inside the mind in the form of experiences. Images are, however, sometimes reconstructive. The impressions gained in a single situation are of course retained but very often few images blend together to form a new image which does not, of course, represent the reality, but becomes a new creation. But even this creation is the result of a background of concrete images.

While impressions take place in the presence of original objects and are results of perception, images occur in the absence of these objects, and are caused by a process of mental reconstruction of an experience undergone. When experiences are varied, there is a danger that before proper impression of an object is formed, a new impression is brought out, and both the impressions get blurred. It is not surprising, therefore, that for a person whose field of experience is limited, the images though few need to be well defined, while a scientist with stray experiences has wide area of floating ideas. This is really an unsatisfactory situation, and its remedy lies in enriching every image with experiences. All persons do not have the same type of impressions. Some seem to be more visual and they receive their impression mostly through the eye, while others may be auditory getting more impressions through the ears. There are persons who receive impression through other senses like the nose, touch or tongue or even through a sense of motion. Which of the senses of a pupil is predominating, can be found by the word or phrase list improvised by Kraplin or Smith. This will help the teacher to plan a course of instruction which may be more useful to a particular student. But this presupposes that instruction should be given either to individual or pupils divided into groups according to their imagery. It has also been seen that persons vary in their imagery. Some persons remember tunes as so many colours, while others remember colours as tunes. Besides these peculiarities, some persons have the remarkable capacity of quick perception. They can recall minute details after a short perception in which a normal person will hardly notice even half of those details.

10

PERSONALITY AND PERSONALITY DEVELOPMENT

What is Personality

Personality like intelligence is a term which is commonly used but its exact definition is yet to be arrived at. Personality is a global concept and it is marked by such characteristics by which a person can be distinguished from others. Generally we take notice of such persons who are able to attract our attention as somewhat different from others. Hypocrites first divided all human beings into four characteristic groups according to their temperament as follows:-

(a) Choleric or those who are easily excitable,

(b) Emotionally feeble and pessimistic or Melancholic,

(c) Emotionally insensitive or Phlegmatic, and

(d) Persevering and optimistic or Sanguine.

According to Hypocrites, these personality differences were caused by certain liver secretions, They affect our emotional life. Centuries after Hypocrites, Willim James in 1911 divided all human beings into two groups: One prone to accept the established ideals whom he called rationalist and the other ready to test and verify things whom he called empiricist. In 1923 Carl Jung had also a two fold division but on a different basis. He called the first group extrovert and held that their standard of judgement and reaction was related to the external world and the other was introvert whose standards were related to the internal or their own inner world.

Allport tried to find personality traits under five broad divisions namely: Intelligence, Motility, Temperature, Self-expression and Sociability. Each of these traits was subdivided into a number of factors. Allport's characteristics are twenty four as follows:—

Intelligence : (a) Capacity to remove obstacles, (b) Memory which is associated with learning, (c) Capacity to see interrelationships, (d) Creative imagination, and (e) Capacity to adjust to new situations.

Motility : (a) Capacity for work, (b) Methods of working, (c) Perseverance, and (d) General Ability.

Temperament : (a) Emotional strength, (b) Breadth or narrowness in the emotional field, (c) Capacity to control one's emotions, (d) Tendencies, and (e) Treatment towards other persons.

Self Expression : (a) Capacity to start work, (b) Insight, (c) Compensatory capacity and capacity to bear loss, (d) Extraversion or introversion, and (e) Aggressive or submissive attitude.

Sociability : (a) Social adjustment, (b) Capacity to share in social activities, (c) Self-centred or Self-evasive attitude, and (d) Character.

While Allport's subdivisions are comprehensive, even if they are somewhat overlapping, its critics hold that the absence of fixed standard for measurements will make allocations subjective and arbitrary.

Some Biological Considerations in determining Personality

Following Hypocrites, Earnest Kretschmer has classified all human beings into biological types, not according to bile secretions but according to their physical structure, and has allotted definite emotional roles associated with each physical make up. These are as follows:-

(a) Pyknics: Short and stout built persons among whom are found potential maniacs and aggressive persons in general.

(b) Asthenics: Tall and thin persons who are generally shy and withdrawing type and among which are found potential schizophrenic persons who suffer from split personality ordinarily talking to themselves.

(c) Athletes, or muscle-built

Researches have shown particularly the fact that there are more maniacs among pyknics and Schizophrenic among Asthenics. Persons end to be stout and well-built and come under the pyknics categorv in an older age and in early youth they are more Asthenic. As prevalence of schizophrenia is mostly in the youth and maniacs are generally found at the age above forty, it is no wonder that he found more maniacs among pyknics and more schizophrenics among Asthenics.

In 1923, Gilbert attempted to divide personality in terms of alkaline secretions and held that aggressive tendencies are measured in terms of the quantity of alkaline secretion. Perman held that if the adrenal glands are over active one becomes more masculine, while if the rear lobes are over active one gets effeminate. An overactive thyroid is more active and persevering. Ross Stagner and Young, however, doubt about Berman's findings stating that our knowledge about the endocrine glands is yet incomplete.

Alfred Adler has, however, deduced certain sociological conclusions. Having found that most of the criminals and deliquents have some physical defects Adler traces the defect as the cause of their maladjustment not only at physical but sociological levels as well. If all persons had defects, then there would be according to him, no tensions. As the handicapped persons suffer from an inferiority complex their behaviour is adversely affected after the tension is thus caused.

Freud's view in Personality Determination

Freud has not denoted any definite personality type as such. He has traced Libido as the basic urge set up by the unconscious tendencies excited by Id. It is sexually inclined. Id which is controlled by Ego or the practical aspect of the self in a normal person. Ego is in its turn controlled by the Super Ego or the moral aspect of the self. Super Ego, according to Freud can not directly control the Id, but it does so always through Ego.

According to Freud, the personality structure is conditioned by the interaction of these forces from early infancy. The libido of a newly born infant is conditioned to its own body, later it gets fixed with its mother. If the fixation and later transference is not normal, it gives an abnormal fixation which Freud has called Oedipus complex. With girls, similar fixation with the father is possible. With the development of age and intellect, the libido is transferred to other persons, at first with persons of the same and later with the opposite sex. According to Freud, the urges of the libido are often running in opposite directions from the activities which are socially approved, and this creates conflicts which the Ego is not able to resolve and thus causes maladjusted personalities.

Freud's findings revolutionised the psychological approach to personalities although all persons do not agree with him. Terman had, for instance, found that instead of attachment to the parents of an opposite sex, boys get more emotionally attached to fathers and girls to mothers. It may further be said that in a joint family-structure in an eastern home, where there are other relatives superior to the parents in a social hierarchy, the findings of Freud would need considerable modification.

Social Influences on Personality Developments

Not only Adler, but a few other psychologists have doubted Freud's conclusions on personality development independent of social forces. Cooley first indicated the influence of the larger society, beyond the child's parents in the determination of personality. William Thomas studied some Polish families which have immigrated in U.S.A. and very soon displayed certain distinct behaviours from what they used to display at Poland. These were consequently the result of the impact of a new social environment. If the behaviours of the refugees from Hungary (after 1956) and of Eastern or Western Pakistan into different States of India, far away from their home-land, are studied we may obtain valuable information about change of personality traits due to social environment. The change is, however, due to three forces, the influence of the older environment, and the influence of the new circumstances.

Anthropologists have found out how certain stereotyped racial characteristics are found in every member of the race, conditioned by the expectations from each individual member of the society. Thus it has been found by Benedict that Zuni Indians of New Mexico, and by Margaret Mead that Tchambulis of New Guinea have more aggressive females and more timid males. The Tharu Indians of Jansar Bawar in U.P. show similar characteristics. All these are conditioned by the respective roles in those lands.

Cyril Burt in England and Eichhorn in Australia have found that most of the delinquents come from broken homes where one of the parents has been divorced or separated, or where the parents are found to be always quarrelling. As opposed to these findings, however, it has been found in U.P., that 80% criminals have come from well adjusted but rather poorer homes. It may be said that in a joint family-structure it is not parents alone that determine the personality development. There are, however, certain tribes in India which were called 'criminal' tribes. They were found to supply the potential criminals. Investigations have found that these have well settled moral codes within their own groups and their so called criminal tendencies are nothing but a sort of hostility to the larger group.

The environment of the school, in addition to home and immediate neighbourhood, no doubt, exerts a considerable influence on the development of the child. Education, no doubt influences the native tendencies of the child. It has been seen that students who have had some education tend to be broad-minded. Contact with one's own age group coming from different families and bringing different family traditions and traits does also help in developing the personality. Then we must not forget the tendency of hero-worship inherent in an adolescent, influencing the personality of the children. An ideal teacher can influence the growth of proper personality. This can easily be seen by comparing children from a good school with those from a bad school. And it is seen that a good family rearing as well as education in a good school are both conducive to a well-integrated personality.

Summary

Human society was concerned with what constitutes a personality. Since physical appearance attracts notice, it was studied first of all, but we find that from the time of Greek civilisation we have not been indifferent to emotional components of the personality as well. There is some definite similarity between what Hypocrites has said about bile secretions and what some of the psychologists say about the secretion of endocrine glands. But our knowledge, then and now, has been incomplete to establish a definite relation between these secretions and development of personality traits. Kretschmer has tried to connect personality traits with body built, but perhaps in this context the explanation given by Alder seems to be more convincing. It is the idea of a social superiority or otherwise that determines these traits. In other words, it is not the traits but their uniqueness in one's group that develops the traits.

Freud has studied the development of personality in terms of the fixation of libido and the adjustment of Id, Ego and Super Ego. His studies have been challenged by others, and may perhaps need some modifications in the light of the observations of eastern families where the upbringing of the child is some-what different.

That the social group from which the children have come had some influence on the personality has been confirmed not only by the study of delinquents coming from broken homes but also from different culture-contexts.

An objective study of the personality whether by Allport or by Benreuter's inventory, interviews or projective techniques give conflicting results, showing that personality being an all pervasive behaviour can not so easily be studied.

Personality and its Measurement

Differential psychology has become perhaps the most active branch of science. But it fails to explore all the dimensions of personality. It is extremely difficult to reach the new horizons of psychology as the personality is too complex to be analysed. Attempt has, however, been made to define personality from various angles. If we make a critical survey of the definitions already attempted, we can classify them under the following categories:-

(a) Omnibus definitions

(b) Configurational definitions

(c) Hierarchical definitions

(d) Definition in terms of adjustment

(e) Definition in terms of distinctiveness.

In spite of all the definitions of the term, it would be worth-while to arrive at a general definition representing a synthesis of contemporary psychology and its usage. The following definition may be accepted as a comprehensive one:-

"Personality is the dynamic organisation within the individual of those psycho-physical systems that determine his unique adjustments to his environment."

The definition represents a synthesis of the speculative thoughts in past ages and much of the scientific research in recent times. Mere definition of the term is not enough for our purposes as we are interested in identifying the elements which constitute personality. Psychology has embraced hopefully many possibilities, faculties, ideas, instincts, factors and dimensions.

Personality is rather an abstraction and character is often used synonymously with it. Some find it more convenient to use 'Temperament" instead of 'Personality'

It is, however, fortunate that almost all the psychologists have taken it as a psycho-physical disposition which develops from the interaction of human impulses. The concept implies certain organised system or structure which is gradually built up and which includes conscious sentiments and interests, complexes or mechanisms and the like.

There have been mainly two kinds of approaches for the assessment of personality for practical purposes.

(1) Typological approach, which can be roughly described as a synthetic approach is more or less concerned with a rough and ready estimate of a person as a whole. The oldest known classification was according to temperaments. It originated with a Greek medical school known as Hypocrite school and was based upon a theory about the varying proportion of four juices or 'humour" in bodies resulting in the following four temperaments.

(a) the Sanguine, (b) the Phlegmatic, (c) the Melancholic, and (d) the Choleric.

The Trait-Composite Approach

This is also an analytic approach and there have been many criticisms against this sort of atomistic study. That personality is a global unit which can by no means be analysed into several component parts, is maintained by few psychologists. But in spite of such vehement protest against the atomistic approach there have been considerable advances made by the factor analysts in this field. According to the former group, mere enumeration of person's traits and habits does not give a complete picture of the person, as the most important aspect of organised structure is ignored thereby. This has been emphatically put forward by Allport who is opposed to the monolithic or analytic approach. On the other hand, psychologists like Eysenck and Cattell have boldly faced the ideographic views but still insist on the necessity for trait-composite approach for practical purposes. It would be idle, according to them, to sit tight with the most vague and subjective approach.

Thus many traits have been discovered and assessments attempted. The term has been defined as a 'Collection of responses bound by some kind of unity which permits the responses to be gathered under a term.'

There have been various types of classifications of such traits as well:-

Unique traits — Common traits,

Surface traits — Source traits,

Constitutional traits — Environmental traits,

Dynamic traits, Ability traits — Temperamental traits, etc.

But among these the most important one is whether the trait is a unitary one or not.

Only recently psychometricians have favoured the conception of elements in terms of factors. The search for such elements has been carried out in many directions. A factor is rather an empirical generalisation. But there are difficulties with this conception of elements.

The first difficulty arises in the naming of factors. These factors very often seem remote from psychological fact and lead to confusion. The basic elements which are supposed to form the fundamental components of personality have unfortunately doubtful existence.

It is, however, assumed that the elements of personality are offered by the theory of pure or independent factors. On the other hand, the theory of focal and overlapping traits suggests the doctrine of functional autonomy. According to those who support functional autonomy, the dynamic substructures are unique and integrated, formed in the individual course of experience and heredity. The factorial approach assumed that they are uniform and they vary in weighages. But this assumption is perhaps mistaken. It is a fact that factorial techniques have some values for certain types of problems in psychology or sociology.

The doctrine of stimulus response elements however holds that personality is made up of a large number of independent characteristics or behaviour-tendencies.

The investigators have proceeded in different lines for exploring personality and discovering the structure of personality.

The problem of organisation and structure of personality is yet to be solved and the structure of personality depends on the consistency of an individual's conduct in an environmental situation.

The theory of partial identity often leads to an answer in the matter of generalisation and integration. It is a very serious question as to whether the inward cohesion in the structure of personality can be accounted for in this way.

The theory of traits is fairly established though they have been regarded as categories for the classification of habits. This is a biosocial approach and the biophysical approach considers a trait as a psychic force determining the active behaviour of an individual. Psychology has never been able to do without some conception of determining tendency and both attitude and trait are indispensable concepts.

The constancy of a trait is nearly an ideal and it is really difficult to discover these traits or assess them for an intimate knowledge of one's personality. To aid in the discovery of common traits a variety of devices is used.

The scientific evidence for the existence of traits comes from its constancy. Most significant of all the attributes of traits and their contribution to the problem of assessment is their interdependence, their uniqueness.

Cattell (1946, 1950, 1957) has made a comprehensive study of investigations into the structure of personality from many sources and different lines of approach. He has developed a theory of personality as a hierarchy of traits: that is collection of reactions or responses which are marked by some kind of unity and by a dynamic (teleological) direction towards a common goal. These traits can be verified and studied by means of correlation clusters and factor analysis. The former method reveals "surface traits", the latter "source traits". In the hierarchy, the basic, primary traits or "constitutional unities", called "urges" include needs and drives, directed towards some biological goal, as well as temperament and aptitude traits. The "environmental mould unities" are directed towards some intermediate goal acquired through the social or physical environment, and these include attitudes, sentiments and interests, which can be resolved into "urges". According to Cattell, attitudes are distinguished from interests through their definition in terms of direction or dynamic feeling (orectic) quality, which he conceives as a measure of the orientation of a vector. Thus, while most attitude tests measure only the orientation through a 180^0 plane-acceptance-rejection, Cattell thinks that many other planes could be used, such as curiosity-incuriosity, acquisitiveness—nonacquisitiveness. What is termed the 'strength' of an attitude is properly a measure of the amount of interest involved. Interest in Cattell's conception is regarded as 'libido-investment'. It will be seen that the distinction could be referred to in the terms of an earlier psychology as that between the affective and conative aspects of such traits.

It follows, therefore, that attitudes, interests and sentiments form a common group of study. In his later work (1957), Cattell affirms that, "Clinical, sociological and general experimental study of attitudes shows them to be linked by sub-goals, forming a lattice."

Four researches planned to test his hypotheses revealed seven well-defined factors having the qualities of drives, and three less clear. In descending order of clarity they were: sex, gregariousness, protectiveness, curiosity, escape, self-assertion, sex-appeal, rest-seeking, and construction. These are ergs. Five fairly well-defined sentiments and two less clear were: sentiment to profession, to sports and games, to religion, to mechanical or material interests, to the self, and possibly the super-ego and patriotic sentiments. He concludes that, on the whole, these represent new factors in a new dynamic modality.

Eysenck (1947, 1953), whose approach has been more from the study of pathological personalities, and who relies, made like Cattell, especially on factor analysis, constructs a hierarchy with four levels. At the 'type' level are three basic factors of neuroticism, introversion-extroversion, and general intelligence or 'g'. At the 'trait' level are such qualities as persistence, rigidity, shyness, etc., and these are related to elements of the third or 'habitual response' level, leading in turn to the 'specific response' level, which, is the lowest one.

In terms of factors, these levels would correspond to general factors, specific factors and error factors. Eysenck points out, however, that throughout the hierarchy, differences are in respect of degrees. The general factor is simply the group factor that is most widespread, while the specific factor is the group factor that is most limited in appeal.

Guilford's book, "personality" (1959), provides a comprehensive approach to the study of personality and an extensive survey of contributions by himself and others to its theory. It is impossible to summarise his conclusions in a few words, but in general it may be said that he accepts the hierarchical conception of personality structure with traits at different levels of generality. First there is the 'Type Level' represented by general social-adjustment types and also general emotional types; below this is the 'Primary-trait Level', the types of which are found by factor analysis, and are exemplified by such qualities as sociability and ascendancy. Next in order is the 'Hexis Level', the term used to describe 'consistent attitudes or dispositions of mind' and at the lowest level are types of specific actions.

Vernon in his recent book "Personality Assessment" has preferred objective study of personality to other approaches, including psycho-analytic one. He admits of the fact that personality is the area too complex and every approach has certain weakness. The propelling forces determining human behaviour are too many. It is, desired that a theory of personality and techniques should be constructed for getting at the right picture of the elements of personality.

We have assumed that personality is a complex whole and the judgement of it is extremely difficult. Still attempts have been made to explore the field from various angles by psychologists who are peripheralists and centralists.

The former group has objective approach, where as the centralists are more concerned with subjective facts of emotional components.

In view of this divergent trend it seems proper to employ a variety of methods for its assessment. There are difficulties that confront the investigator of personality. There are objective and subjective facts standing in the way. For example, the changing conditions of the physical and social environment, the changing physiological conditions within the subject, the motivational trends and patterns of the subject deserve special mention.

Similarly reports given by the subject of his perceptions, interpretations, feelings are subjective facts which influence the scientific study of personality.

In short, it may be said that variables of personality and the approaches made so far to study them are numerous. Very recently psycho-analysis has been tried for exploring this domain.

The unconscious level of personality organisation is now being attacked with the assumption that the psychic process involved has great resolving power when applied to the mysterious phenomena underlying personality structure. According to Murray, a need is a hypothetical process, the occurrence of which is imagined in order to account for certain objective and subjective facts.

Here, of course, emphasis has been laid not on the overt behaviour but on the inner conflicts, feelings, emotions, sentiments and beliefs.

Introspection and experiments demonstrate that an emotion basically determines the cognitive process underlying any behaviour pattern.

Thus need is a dynamic concept which has been formulated by Murray for explaining the mysteries of human behaviours. McDougall's instinct theory has thus been outdated by the theory of need.

The advantages of dealing with unitary traits, do not reduce the difficulties in their identification.

In spite of outstanding problems in the area of assessments, the 'factor analytic' technique has made a move in a definite direction. Few unitary traits have been established by cattell, Eysenck and others. The degree of success in a certain occupation or school subject partly depends upon intelligence and partly upon personality qualities. This is why the need for research on personality and its assessments is being felt more and more in recent times.

PERSONALITY MEASUREMENT

Personality is too complex to be analysed. There have been various attempts for measuring personality from different angles:-

(1) Subjective : method of impression.

(2) Objective : method of expression.

Of the subjective approaches, the following deserve mention: (a) ratings, (b) interview, (c) self-rating or questionnaire.

Of the objective approaches, situational tests deserve special mention. Besides, projective tests are being evolved for depth study of personality.

In spite of every attempt at the assessment of personality, much remains to be explored in this field. It appears that the various dimensions of personality have not yet been discovered as yet and the techniques so far evolved are not adequate.

Ratings

The objective of the rating method is to derive knowledge, about a person through others estimates and to turn them into numerical grades or scores. The subjectivity of judgements of personality is apparent. Ratings are therefore, regarded as grades obtained in specific areas on the reputation of the subject. They are however, inadequate as the sole criteria of a person's traits, or even as the entire source of date for the scientific study of personality.

There are various rating techniques, viz. ranking, paired comparisons, numerical ratings, verbal, graphic and other analytic scales.

Ranking and paired comparisons

This technique is advantageous when the number of cases is very limited. In the paired comparison method, the rater is given every possible pair of names and asked to say which of the two is higher.

Numerical Ratings

The outstanding defect of this type of scale is the variation in standard and distribution adopted by different raters.

But this is a very simple pattern. There is no really satisfactory way of comparing the ratings by different judges of different groups and this greatly limits the practical value of rating.

(a) Verbal and Graphic Scales

In the graphic scale each step is defined or described as concretely as possible, so that the rater no longer has to think quantitatively or bother about standards.

(b) Analytic Scales

This is the device of breaking up a general trait into a number of more specific components, which are separately rated and scores combined. In the marking of essays analytic schemes are often found to be no more reliable than impressionistic.

A number of steps have been taken to increase the reliability of ratings, i.e. agreement between different raters. It has been considered that there is the superiority of relative to absolute and of graphic to numerical ratings. There are definite advantages of breaking down traits into components. The following suggestions have been made by the psychologists:-

1. Choose only the unambiguous traits and find them correctly.
2. Rate all individuals on one trait at a time
3. Warn the raters of the personal bias and encourage them to be objective by obtaining independent judgements.
4. Ratings should be based on sample observations for a definite period.

Interview

Interview is the most comprehensive of all methods as it is based on observations of external appearance, gesture, other modes of expression and various behaviour patterns revealed during the interview. The reliability and validity of interview as a technique is not very satisfactory and it should therefore, be supplemented by other tests.

Interviews may vary in types. There may be individual interview, psychiatric interview and group interviews. Each has its value and limitations. So far as assessment of personality is concerned, the impressions, gathered in short interview, are hardly dependable. Interview may put an interviewees under considerable strains and yet the interviewers are liable to make wrong judgements.

Self-ratings

Ratings by the individuals of their own traits are known as self-ratings. This technique is popularly known as questionnaire. The questionnaires are easy to construct and use. In questionnaire, the responses of the subjects can be obtained in writing. This is why this technique has been widely used. So far as personality tests are concerned, the outstanding tests are those of Burnreuter, Cattell, Guildford and Eysenck. The main difficulty in using personality inventories or questionnaires is that the subject may either consciously or unconsciously fake his answers. Vernon concludes that despite the extreme weaknesses of questionnaires, they should not be entirely condemned. Well constructed questionnaires effectively administered in suitable motivating conditions can be of value both for experimental research or for clinical use.

Situational Tests

These tests are more objective in nature as the subject is unaware of the scoring system employed and consequently unable to guess the purpose of the test as well. The subjects are placed in miniature situations provided for obtaining their responses. But this may lead to considerable difficulty because of the subject's over awareness of the artificial situations. Although the validity of such personality tests varies widely the science of personality assessment is enriched by such objective tests of situational type.

The Projective Test

The projective technique holds its promise in playing an important part in personality assessment. This approach was adopted largely as a revolt against superficial testing of personality. Insight into the personality as a whole has been considered to be the primary objective of such a test. The advantage of a projective test is that the subject cannot guess the purpose of the test which brings out many unconscious urges and motives, traits and tendencies. The difficulty in applying such a test is that it demands skill and insight on the part of the experimenter. Rorschach's ink blocks and T.A.T. are the most outstanding tests in this field. Besides, other techniques of exploring the personality at the unconscious level have been evolved such as free word association, story telling test, object relation test, etc.

11

EXERCISE AND METHODS OF LEARNING

We all seem to know what constitutes learning. Yet a controversy may arise about its scientific definition, as all are not agreed as to what learning constitutes and the manner in which one may learn.

Associationist Conception

Associationists believe that when a new experience is brought about, our mind tries to locate its similarity with some thing familiar, something it has seen or known before and then to associate or connect the new fact with that old experience. This method, according to the associationists, produces certain economy. Instead of remembering so many isolated experiences one has to remember only few bundles of experiences whose connections are based on certain similarity or association. Disconnected items of knowledge may be too numerous to create confusion. But when grouped in a certain order they are like bundles of books arranged in a shelf and can be recalled when needed.

According to associationists, therefore, learning takes place when the mind is able to see the relationship between the new knowledge and the old. It is only when association of the new knowledge with the old one has taken place, learning is possible. Some associationists will go one step further. They would find in this mechanism not only better learning for the new items of information, but a better definition of the older one.

When a new boy enters the class, we try to recall the similarity he has with some person whom we have seen before. In doing so, we shall at the same time notice the points of dissimilarity. This improves our knowledge of the old and familiar things and also making them better defined. This is a process by which new things become known, and old things also get better known. This is known as the process of apperception.

Associations can be changed. They may be accidental, logical and systematic. Supposing I go to Delhi on a wet day when it is raining hard, my impressions of Delhi will always be associated with the rains, and perhaps my impression of Delhi will be that it is a wet place. As a matter of fact, this is merely accidental as Delhi has more dry days in the year than we think and the rainfall is not at all heavy. Yet because of the mere accident of my going there on a wet day, my association of Delhi will be with a wet place. My impressions will always be biased and wrong due to this accidental association. Many of our associations get biased because of the influence of chance factor.

But all our associations are fortunately not accidental. Often we reason out connections and find out relationship. According to associationists, therefore, learning is perfect if the associations are natural and meaningful.

Behaviourists' Conception

The psychologists who place more reliance on the behaviour that a living being displays when placed in a new situation are called behaviourists. Unlike the associationist who looks into the problem from the point of view of subject matter, behaviourist places more reliance on the responses, made by the learner himself. When a new situation confronts a living being, it is natural that he will try to react to it. So long as these reactions are disorganised and random lead no desired end, no learning takes places. Learning, according to the behaviourists, is the organised response that is conditioned or practised by the learner. They would further find out a reason why a learner practises. It is because the response helps in the adjustment of the learner to his environment. The behaviourists will draw some line of distinction between automatic responses like the reflex action of closing one's eyelid and responses that are chosen and organised. Automatic responses are not learnt and they show very little improvement, as they involve no organisation. Some psychologists would go one step further, and say that the slight extent to which some of the automatic responses are improved by practice shows the slight degree of organisation that is involved in them.

The behaviourists have brought forward the famous conditioned response theory. We owe it to the classical experiment of Pavlov. This Russian Psychologist had trained his dog in a peculiar way. Every day exactly sixty seconds after the ringing of a bell he would serve the dog with a dish of meat. One day, after many days of repeated practice, he did not bring the meat and observed the reaction of the dog to the sound of the bell. He found that as soon as the bell was rung, the dog became somewhat alert, but his mouth did not begin watering then. It was just sixty seconds after the sound of the bell that the dog's mouth watered, as if it was expecting its food then. Thus he found that the dog has connected or conditioned its response to two stimuli with which the object of its interest, the food, was connected. It knew that the sound of the bell had something to do with it and therefore, learnt to be alert.

But it also knew the implication of the time interval of sixty seconds, as then and then only the appropriate response, the watering of the mouth was visible.

The followers of the Conditioned Response Theory hold that learning in its fundamental form is essentially a modification of all natural responses, and their transference to artificial stimuli. In this particular case of Pavlov Experiment, the natural response of the accumulation of saliva, was connected not with the arrival of food, but with the artificial stimuli, namely with the sound of the bell, and the time interval of sixty seconds.

Being a physiological theory, conditioned response at once commends itself to those who want an objective but at the same time a physiological basis of the process of learning. According to this theory, a natural response may be modified by bracketing it with an artificial response and they together form a certain action which, may be called a reflex action. The response is simultaneous, as in the case of watering of the mouth at the very name of the delicious food, but sometimes we may modify the situation as in the case of ringing of the bell sixty seconds before the serving of the food. Here because of the time interval which has been inevitably followed, we find the response is consequently delayed. It does not occur at the mere ringing of the bell. This is clearly the case of a delayed response.

Followers of this theory hold that conditioning often takes place in our childhood and although the natural causes are forgotten, the effects or the response patters still remain. Childhood fears are thus result of conditioned response, e.g., fears for certain harmless animal like spiders and cockroaches often shown by adults. We may remember them as the results of conditioning of certain childhood experiences which have perhaps been forgotten. Perhaps these 'meaningless' fears display a meaning of their own. What has thus been done by accident can be done deliberately by an educator. If the educator wants a desirable type of responses, all he must do is to condition or arrange appropriate situations. The child will then respond in the way we desire him to respond. By repeated practice this response will be so conditioned that the response becomes apparently automatic. Learning thus becomes the process of habit. It is the educator, the teacher, who has to do all planning and arranging of situations in order to get a type of response that he desires. His task again is to arrange for repeated practice so that the response becomes ingrained.

The theory, no doubt, gives a plausible account of conditions of specific learning, particularly, in those situations which involve a certain amount of emotional response. It, however, fails to explain the cases of complex thought processes.

Thorndike's Laws

Thorndike also bases this conception of learning on the stimulus response theory, but he would add two more factors of requisites to the mere practice effect that brings about learning. Thorndike would try to look into the reason why a certain living being becomes ready to receive the stimulus at all and why he would act.

The subject would be ready to receive the stimulus only when such response brings a certain amount of pleasure. Satisfaction is, therefore, the first and foremost condition of learning. Without it no individual will react to the stimulus at all. Happiness derived from the response forms the motive force.

Thus the stimulus and the response should be related to one another. It is only when there is a natural connection between the way of acting and the result aimed at, an individual is motivated to repeat or carry on the process and learn.

Besides these two fundamental facts, Thorndike would add another condition to the very practice. The more recent has been the practice, the greater would be the learning effect.

The first solution of an adjustment according to Thorndike takes place in simple trial and error process. A rat kept inside a box which has a hole in it, will jump at random to get out. It is by mere accident that he hits upon the particularly favourable place from where he may get out if he jumps again. If he is taken into the box again, he will perhaps need fewer attempts to hit at the right place. And finally as soon as he is put into the box, he comes to the right spot wherefrom he can make a successful attempt to escape.

Analysing the situation, we find that the rat's first attempt involves a process of mere trial and error. He tried several places and made few errors before he came to the right spot from where he could jump successfully. This gave him the freedom, which is a pleasurable sensation.

Next time when the rat is put into the box he was motivated to try the process. Gradually he eliminates his unnecessary and unsuccessful jumps because he finds a connection between the action namely jumps, and the attainment of his goal, viz., freedom. This connection naturally involves a selection of the site and both the practice and the pleasure sensation of freedom provides stimulation. Further, if time elapses it is likely that the rat would forget the thing he learnt, and would have to repeat the process with unnecessary jumps before he hits the right spot again.

Thus Thorndike mentions four conditions for learning and provides that the learning to be effective should depend on certain laws which are as follows:-

(a) **Law of Frequency :** The more frequent is the practice, the greater will be the learning effect. Here Thorndike does not differ from the followers of the Conditioned Reflex Theory who also believe that it is practice that makes one perfect.

(b) **The law of effect :** If the situation motivates the learner it would provide greater chance of learning. While Thorndike takes away from the educator the right of determining which situations and stimuli are to be selected, the followers of Conditioned Response Theory would, give the choice of action to the learner. This places a greater responsibility on the educator, for he has to select not only desirable but desired situations.

(c) **The law or Recency :** The more recent is the practice, the greater would be the chance of learning. In this Thorndike has stated a thing which the followers of the Conditioned Reflex Theory might have implied but have never expressed. Any way, there is no variation in two theories with reference to this.

(d) **Law of Belongingness :** In order to motivate practice further, both the stimulus and the response must be connected or should belong to one another. In this too, Thorndike merely completes what the followers of Conditioned Reflex Theory have left unsaid. Surely the response in order to be conditioned, must belong or must be connected with the stimulus. But the connection has not been clearly stated in so many words as a necessary requirement for learning.

Gestalt View of Learning

Gestalt psychologists like Kohler and Koffka held that mental phenomena have a certain structure or pattern. The standpoint of the associationists had been to assume that individual items stand apart from each other, but this is not the case. A Gestalt psychologist does not look in to isolated items; he looks in to the total pattern or configuration. When we are looking at a certain individual or individual object, we are not unmindful of the total perspective in which that individual or the object happens to exist for the time being. Perhaps we are for the moment paying a greater attention to the particular individual. Yet the background effect the total panorama produces should not be overlooked. Ideas do not come to us in isolation. They are really parts of a total pattern or context by virtue of which they acquire a certain meaning and significance. According to this theory, when we learn a poem, we do not learn the individual words or lines of the poem but try to read the poem as a whole (or at least a significant portion of it which we may call a unit). This forms a complete unit of thought. If we happen to forget a particular line or stanza, the prompter just supplies the catchword and at once the whole chain of subsequent thoughts flashes back into mind. Why is it that supply of a single word helps us to recall the entire stanza? The followers of Gestalt School of thought would say that it is because the whole chain of words that form the stanza is so intimately connected (and the learning of the particular catch word has been so well knit with this chain) that the supply of the catch word helps us to call back into the mind the entire situation. The word in which stands out the midst of the chain of words is in the stanza.

Gestalt school of psychologists objects to the formulation or the problem of learning as implied by the four laws of Thorndike. Thorndike's basic position has been to find the connection between the stimulus and the response. These laws assume that for independent stimuli there are independent units of behaviour. Followers of the Gestalt do not believe in such isolated units. When we look at a certain scene, we have already organised our response to the total situation. What we call perception or learning, according to the followers of the Gestalt is the discovery of the relationships that exists between the elements on which we focus or concentrate our attention. Learning is thus not a building up of a wall by piling up bricks. It is the excavation of a huge mound to trace the hidden treasure. Gestalt theory assumes that learning takes place in a total situation and not in piece meal. In order to learn a poem it is easier to take the entire piece than to take it line by line or stanza by stanza, provided it is of a reasonable length. In case of longer poems also it is desirable to take one complete and meaningful unit of thought which may serve as the focal reference point. Learning by part proves less effective than learning by whole.

Dewey's Conception of Learning

According to John Dewey and his followers, learning is possible only when the individual feels a need for it. All learning according to him is purposeful taking place in the direction in which the purpose is being fulfilled. Ordinarily we do not observe how many cracks a wall has got, unless we are interested in its repair or are afraid of the wall collapsing. In both these situations, however, we are likely to observe minutely and when we do so, learning takes place. Dewey further assumes that when learning is taking place, an individual is participating in the situation as a single undivided organism. When we are playing, we are certainly interested in winning the game. We have thus an interest which motivates our action. Our entire organism, the body and the mind, are engaged together in this activity. It is in this type of situation where direct participation is possible, maximum learning takes place. This Dewey would call primary learning.

Dewey, however, admits that there is a scope for a different type of learning in certain situations where direct participation of the individual is not possible. Facts of the remote past or of distant lands can not be given in any other way except through a certain amount of communication. But whenever such communication is taking place, the actual learning that takes place is not much unless some opportunity for participation is provided. There is yet a third type of learning which may be the result of drawing inferences or conclusions from a topic learnt.

But here the situation should be presented in the form of a problem and the individual must feel the need for solving the problem.

Thus like Thorndike, Dewey believes in the law of readiness in as much as he recognises the need for motivation in learning situations. Dewey, however, places more reliance on the cause of motivation rather than on the effect. The goal must be worthwhile but pleasure would lie in the pursuit rather than in the attainment. The urge for pursuit, he feels, would come only when there is a felt need. He would further agree with Thorndike to the idea of belongingness. The situation should be meaningful, and the pursuit should take place in the direction of attainment. Both the goal and the significance of the effort in the direction of reaching the goal must be clear in the mind of the learner.

Like Kohler an Koffka, Dewey feels that learning does not take place by mere blind repetition or by thoughtless trial and error. He would modify Thorndike's law of exercise to the extent that exercise and repetition at each instance must be purposeful. Each renewed effort must be caused in such situations where there is a fresh motivation created in fulfilling one's need. Each exercise must be both purposeful and meaningful. One can not moreover learn in piecemeal. It is possible that we may concentrate on one aspect of the total process, but the background of the total situation is to be kept in view. Experience can not be subdivided into narrow compartments. Real learning takes place through the reaction of the organism to the whole and not part situations. There are of course certain focal points, but these are taken by the learner as mere means to reach the goal.

Summary

Opinion seems to be divided regarding the process through which a living organism tries to learn and gain better control over its surroundings. What it learns becomes helpful as it ensures an economy in future encounters by reducing the random effort which are noticeable in early efforts. Association shows that there is a certain economy if the new things learnt can be properly connected with a thing learnt in the past. It is only when the old and new get connected or associated, our ideas about the old things become clearer. The followers of this theory held that such association, may be quite accidental or deliberately planned and organised. They would, however, place more reliance on deliberate associations.

One school of behaviourist would place more reliance on Conditioned Response or Condition-Reflex Theory. Learning, according to them, takes place by repetition of process, when the connections between stimulus and response become ingrained. The followers of this theory would place all the responsibility for arranging the suitable situation and evoking desired response on the teacher or educator. It is for him to organise such situations and repeat the process so that learning may take place.

Thorndike, while admitting that sometime learning takes place by blind repetition or mere trial and error, would at the same time emphasize value of satisfaction derived. In other words, the outcome of learning situation should give some degree of satisfaction or pleasure (as pointed out in his law of effect).

He takes a commonsense view that the practice must be recently done, otherwise things learnt in the remote periods may be lost. He holds that the goal and the effort must be clear before the learner.

Kohler, Koffka and other followers of the Gestalt school feel that learning does not take place from parts to whole but rather from the whole to the part. Learning is not a building up process like piling up of bricks of information. It is the development of insight that comes into the mind of the learner to discover the relationships that exist between the particular parts of the situation for which the total situation stands as background.

Dewey's view of learning takes some thing from Thorndike and some thing from the Gestalt School. He also feels the need for belongingness and pleasure sensation. But according to him, the source of pleasure is not the attainment of the goal but really the effort. The individual must feel that his pursuit is worthwhile. This is possible only when the individual is conscious of the need for learning or exertion. He also agrees with the Gestalt school in considering the total pattern or background to which the individual learner acts as a single undivided being. But while an individual is interested in the total situation, he may yet select certain focal points for attacks. This will, however, be done so long as the particular focal point is connected with the main objective. Dewey makes a distinction between three types of learning. The first is one in which direct participation is possible. This is called primary learning situations which provide opportunity for Gestalt learning. But he admits that when direct participation is not possible, there is room for communication as well as for drawing inferences and conclusions. These are secondary and Primary learning situations and the degree of possible success in such situations depends on how they can be organised.

It may be profitable at this stage to look into the learning process that Dashiell has prepared to study the different conditions of learning, so as to make our study objective :—

The subject must be motivated. We can take an example from a simple experiment of maze learning of a rat. If we keep the food inside a maze and lead a rat through it to secure the food, he will not go and seek the food unless he is hungry. A well-fed rat may fall asleep at the door of the maze. It is only the hungry rat that explores and eventually finds his way. Dashiell thus agrees with Dewey that learning takes place in meaningful situations.

There must be some obstruction or barrier of some sort without which no learning takes places. In the above instance, if the food is supplied at the very entrance of the maze, where is the opportunity of the rat for learning? We thus find that through easy situation there is hardly any learning. There must be some obstacle to be felt as the same provides a motive force.

In every learning situation, the first movements are random and varied. This is seen not only in animal experiments but also in a complex situation as when one is learning to drive a car. Trial and error being the most fundamental process are gradually organised into definite patterns of behaviour.

Successful responses come mostly by chance. In learning by trial and error. or by conditioning perhaps the subject can not predict the results. In one, he hits accidentally and in the other he is made to do certain action at the dictation of another person. Hence in both these situations, the benefit of gaining an insight through the chance situation is perhaps lost. When, however the subject is conscious and alert, perhaps he will find a new meaning to the chance occurrence and this is called insight.

It is the effect that determines how an individual would select or fix the right responses. When a certain activity leads to a desired goal, the attainment brings some satisfaction. The connection between the effort made for its attainment and the goal itself proves meaningful so that learning takes place. Better motivation is perhaps possible when each repetition of the process brings some added satisfaction.

Learning may come rapidly or it may take a long time. When insight occurs, there is a sudden improvement. With trial and error and with conditioning there is progress no doubt, but the progress is slow.

Since learning depends on sense perception, loss or defect of any sense affects improvement of knowledge in that direction.

The common assumption that the blind hears better or the deaf sees better is not borne by facts. True it is that there is some compensation, but in its totality, the loss is greater than the slight gain.

Any fatigue, whether muscular or mental retards learning. Over-exertion must, therefore, be prevented and the physical conditions of ventilation or illumination must be satisfactory to provide freedom from physical fatigue.

Frequent practice given at regular internal is better than one long and continuous practice. It is better to repeat the process for ten minutes a day than to have one practice of two hours once in six days. This is, however, conditioned by the fact that such practice should be in complete units to be learnt at a time.

Age and maturity must be taken into account as well. Two experiments on identical twins offer good instance of this. Two identical twins are made to climb a few steps. The practice for the first was begun in the forty-six week, but for other it was delayed till the child was fifty-two weeks old. When the second child began its practice, it was seen that the first had already acquired some practice. In the 53rd week the first child could climb first steps in twenty six seconds while the second took forty-five seconds to do so.

Seven weeks later both the children took the same time. Thus though the second child had only eight weeks practice, yet it was equal to the former's fourteen week practice simply because the former began when it was still immature.

A review of the Theories of Leaning

Learning is a continuous process leading to improvement of behaviour. Various theories of learning have emerged. All these theories are based on certain observations. Some of them have been developed from behaviouristic standpoint, while others are the result of certain principles. Thus the principle of association of ideas has given rise to the traditional theory of association in learning, whereas the learning has also been explained in a more mechanical manner, viz, in terms of (connectionism) stimulus response. The latter approach emphasises the mechanical process by which bonds are built, strengthened and organised into systems. When applied in the field of education, this theory encouraged the educators to think of ways and means for creating S.R. bonds. Thorndike's laws of learning were enunciated for the purpose. But they could not explain the complex process of human learning. Modern theories by Hull and Tolman were evolved. Hull's theory of reinforcement springs from the law of effect and the concept of conditioning combined together. Tolman's theory of sign learning emphasised the importance of meaning in learning. Trial and error methods of learning have a much better place in Hall's theory while motivation, rewards and punishment have been regarded as signs helping the learning process in Tolman's theory.

Thus Tolman's view is very rational and adequate in accounting for human learning. In short, Tolman's theory links up the mechanism of early learning with the complex learning process observed in classroom situation. Hull has contributed to the theory of learning by introducing learning as conditioning and emphasising the role of need reduction for reinforcement of the S.R. connection. But Hull's theory has a number of limitations which were rightly pointed out by Tolman. It was Tolman who has tried to make an advance in the theory of learning by giving credit for insightful learning for signs and meanings.

It appears, that behaviouristic school of psychology explains learning in the light of the experience of animal behaviour. The behaviourists has deliberately avoided the role of experience in learning and attached no importance to the mental function, like intention and willingness in learning.

Thus there are serious limitations in the theories of learning, emerging from the behaviouristic school of psychology. The various laws of effect, conditioning and reinforcement presuppose a mechanical set-up in the learner. Though the question of reinforcement cannot be fully explained without any reference to intent and experience, a part explanation has only been sought by a haphazard interpretation of trial and error in the light of need reduction. A concept of conditioning ignores the motivational aspect of learning and is thus subject to criticism. It is unfortunate that a tendency towards oversimplification of the complex learning process has led to the development of theories almost in a mechanical manner. But there are certain characteristics of complex human achievements calling for a more comprehensive theory of learning. The role of experience, intention and insight, of criticism and construction and of generalisation of learning is to be taken into account while building up a rational theoretical framework in this field.

Human experience in perception and cognition plays a very prominent part in learning. Gestalt psychology is concerned with the problem of perception, which has been almost ignored by the behaviouristic school. Human perceptual experience cannot be fully explained in terms of pure sensation. There is something more which remains to be discovered. In any learning or perception the quality of each component is determined with reference to the whole. In Wertheimer's words, the characteristics of any Gestalt are determined not only by its parts but also by internal arrangement.

So far as the formation of Gestalt is concerned, Wertheimer holds that there are various perceptual phenomena in the visual field. The laws underlying the formation of Gestalts or whole configurations and the factors which influence their formation deserve special mention.

According to Koffka, configurations tend to become as clear as the conditions permit. A good form implies units, harmony inclusiveness and consciousness. There are several factors contributing to the formation of a good gestalt such as similarity and proximity of elements. Besides this, closure and clarity facilitate gestalt formation. These help one to organise perceptual situations through experience and to promote the learning situation of the classroom by means of stimulating cognition. In the whole process of perception, cognition and learning, in relation to any learning situation, a very important factor known as 'insight' creeps in. As in the course of experience by repetition, analogy, analysis and practice, the parts become related to each other and insight becomes clearly structural. A constant organisation and reorganisation in the perceptual field goes on in order to find improved means for reaching a goal. This character of insightful behaviour is one of the most important features in effective learning.

Insight of course calls for the intellectual ability in the learning. Hillgard gives a list of characteristics of insightful learning.

In early learning by insight it is important that all aspects of the problem situation are accessible and the learning process can be used in new situations. In short, the underlying principle of Gestalt psychology is that each individual is active in his effort so as to organise and give good structure to his learning with the derived satisfaction. Judd in his experiments has shown the importance of generalisation and verbalisation in any learning. In his own opinion, verbalising insight can lead to enhanced structuring. Insight may be aided by modelling the abstract knowledge.

In conclusion, it may be said that learning as insight has been as a concept much indebted to the theory of Gestalt psychologists, like. Koffka and Kohler as the problem of insight is closely connected with perception.

12

TRANSFER OF TRAINING

Developments of the Faculty Theory

The field of learning is vast and if we want learning to be really useful, we shall certainly wish that whatever power or faculty has been developed through the learning situation in one field should be useful in many other fields. If the school teaches a boy to be honest, it certainly does not like to limit the exercise of that quality only inside the examination hall, for instance. The boy should be honest in every walk of life, whether he works as a cashier in a firm or as a judge in a court. If the training given in school situations is not applicable in life situations it should be considered as insufficient or ineffective.

Thus a certain amount of transfer is not only desirable but is necessary. The subject matter of a particular study and the specific power that the study develops are no doubt, connected. The study of certain subjects facilitates preparation for studying a few other subjects. A little grounding in mathematics is necessary to understand the principles of physical sciences or statistics.

The idea that the study of certain subjects confers on the learner certain specific powers is as old as Plato. It was Plato who said that arithmetic sharpens wit and geometry increases the power of apprehension or general understanding of a situation. In other words, a study of arithmetic not only makes a person better able to compute (calculate) quantitative proportions, but it has an additional use of making a person witty. Likewise, the study of geometry in addition to developing powers to distinguish shapes also enables a student to understand or grasp any similar situation. A person is thus advised to study logic when one is not able to differentiate.

John Locke formulated the theory in a logical manner and propounded what is known to day as the transfer theory. Locke supposed that the study of certain subjects can develop certain faculties like memory, reasoning, power of judgement. Study of mathematics, it was supposed, develops the reasoning power, while study of a classical subject is helpful to train our imaginative powers. Other curricular subjects in a like manner were considered by him helpful to develop certain other faculties.

It was felt that the development of the faculty was the primary concern while the knowledge of content of a particular study was considered to be less important. The process of learning thus gained more importance than the content. Training in a particular subject is considered as a mere means to an end. What was being taught was of little significance by itself. Whether the subject matter was of any practical value, whether it was connected with life or not became matters of little consideration. Pupil's interest was not the criterion for relation of the subject matter. The pupil's mind has to be properly disciplined. Thus the faculty theory developed the theory of Formal Discipline.

Many modern educators feel that this theory of Locke has set back the wider interest of education in many ways:-

1. It has helped the retention of some of the less useful subjects in the curriculum. After the development of the modern European languages as a result of Renaissance, subjects like Latin has lost their practical utility in every-day life and would have perhaps been studied by few research workers. It was Locke's Faculty theory that justified their retention in the curriculum. As subjects for study they were no longer useful, having lost the utility of international communication and their place was taken by the modern language like English and French.

2. Though of great practical utility, the study of scientific subjects was delayed for a long time, simply because the educators could not agree as to what particular faculty of mind would their study develop. Even when they were eventually introduced in the curriculum they were taught in a formal and logical manner. More attention was paid to the method of teaching than to the content taught.

3. No effort was made to make the curriculum useful or interesting. Because of the supposed disciplinary value, they were just imposed upon the pupils.

The present educators, therefore, do not follow this theory blindly.

Limited Transfer Theory

As the studies in social and natural sciences developed, it was clear that the study of these subjects were found to be vital to our every day life. They were considered to have certain intrinsic values of their own, apart from the values of training of certain faculties.

Psychology essentially ceased to be a speculative subject when it acquired an experimental character. Psychologists would then like to perform experiments and ascertain objectively whether any transfer has taken place at all or not. Between 1800 and 1928, as many as ninety-nine experiments have been performed in a recognised manner, on the problem of transfer of training to see whether training given in one situation could be effectively transferred into another situation. James performed experiments on memory. A group of subjects was asked to memorise a certain thing, while, another group containing pupils of equal ability were left free. After a time both the groups were asked to memorise another thing, say another poem. Now if the first group would show better efficiency, one may conclude that their earlier act of memorizing has been effective, otherwise, the power of remembering had not been transferred from the first to the second situation. Others performed similar experiments on other learning abilities. By means of an experimental group which was made to learn something and by a control group which did not get a chance of learning, their learning ability in a new situation was tested. It was found that in 32 cases there was an evidence of considerable transfer. In 49 cases the transfer was just partial. In eight cases the transfer was so insignificant that it could be neglected and in five cases there was positive proof that no transfer had taken place. In the remaining five cases it was difficult to predict whether any transfer had taken place at all or not.

In short, in two out of six cases there is a positive proof of appreciable transfer. In three cases the transfer is only partial, while in one case either there is no transfer, or it is quite insignificant. This simply points to the fact that transfer is, on the whole, possible only to a limited extent.

We may now analyse the conditions and find out which factors would decide whether a transfer would take place or not. When the situation is identical either in the procedure or in the attitude, we find that a transfer is possible. Thorndike, for instance, found that when a person was made to learn two poems one after another and these poems had same metre or they conveyed a similar thought, then the effect of learning the first was transferred into the second so that the second was learnt quickly. Judd found that practice in solving one kind of problems helps the learner to solve other kinds of problems so long as the basic situation of problem solving remains the same. When one is working on simultaneous equation in Algebra for instance, he will acquire some power over the problem solving of a different type of simultaneous equation. He will need additional practice for working with certain other features of problem solving. It is on account of this that we do find that even in a new type of problem, one who has solved problems of any kind has a certain advantage.

Insight into a configuration (shape) or general perception of patterns are possibly transferred. So are good habits of work, neatness and orderliness. But these are only partially transferred.

Criticism of the Partial Transfer Theory

Even this theory of limited transfer is not free from criticism. Many psychologists hold that Thorndike's identical element theory does not really show or prove that there has been a transfer. When the elements are identical, what has happened is merely repeated exercise. It is agreed on all sides that repeated exercise helps retention and that learning is re-inforced by practice. The so-called 'new situation' is merely a recapitulation of the old element. For example if a boy has learnt the English words. 'Revolve' and he next learns the Latin root 'Volva' i.e. to roll, he is not learning really a new word but transferring the power acquired from his knowledge in English. He is really practising the basic elements of English word for a second time and when this additional practice is given there is some gain.

They likewise find fault with Judd's experiments, and show that a student clear in solving algebric problems does not show the same competence in solving a problem in Economics. There is no general ability of problem solving.

They are merely specific fields, and in each field larger the number of problems solved, the greater is the practice and quicker gets the speed for solving future problems.

Kohler working with apes found that the more intelligent ones solved their problems of food procurements, by a sudden insight when confronted with certain obstruction. He concludes that the content of the total situation or configuration is subconsciously visualised by the ape. All the while he is trying to concentrate on a specific aspect of the situation that is presented to him in a problematic form. Apparently, the ape was idle, but really he was actively engaged in manipulating the total situation in general. He managed to succeed in his attempt at solving the specific aspect, as a matter of course. An experiment was performed with four hens, three apes and a child, each of whom had to procure the food from a box. In each case he kept the food inside a box which we may call 'B' and which appeared to be somewhat lightly compared to another box 'A' which did not contain any food. After a number of practices each of the subjects learnt how to procure food from the box 'A' and the experimenter by altering the position of the boxes made this recognition well established. Then he quietly changed the box A and replaced it by another 'C' which happened to be more brightly coloured than the box 'B'. It was found that all subjects invariably tried to find the food in box 'C' and not in the box B. This clearly shows that the subjects did not recognise the box B at all, what they did is to learn that the food was in the brighter one of the two boxes. So long as B remained the brighter of the two, there was no difficulty. This experiment thus shows that with a change in the situation, learning loses its value. Thus transfer from one field to another is doubtful. Learning and perception in relation to the whole field of experience and the entire field situation can hardly be repeated in toto.

Our present Theory

Today we seem to doubt the very theory of identical elements put forward by Thorndike, as two fields can not be entirely identical. Apparently the old law of exercise is being presented in another form. As a matter of fact, similarity of two situations gave the learner some advantage by affording him a chance of practice. Thus the theory of transfer is challenged in certain quarters.

If, however, the subject-matter be adopted to the intellectual level of the learner, a certain amount of insight helps in broadening and generalising the zone of perception. This is not really a case of transfer. As, a new situation is interpreted in the light of past experiences of a similar situation, the past experience gives a new meaning to the situation and facilitates successful encounter with the new situation.

It is, however, found that certain routine habits formed by mechanical practice may persist or may be recalled for use. It is thus a case of recall of identical elements or added opportunity for practice. In language study for instance, grammar and spelling form the routine habit which can be taken from one situation and be used in a similar situation. Certain desirable attitudes, dispositions, methods of attack, ideals of accuracy, neatness and social values like honesty may be inculcated generally, and are capable of wide applications in similar situations.

Summary

Need for wider application of desirable habits taught in school to life situations is generally felt. This at first gave birth to the faulty-faculty theory, started by Plato and followed by Locke. The limitation of this theory has been found as it leads to the retention of useless subjects in the curriculum, utter neglect of the content of the curriculum and indifference to children's natural urges. With the introduction of social and natural sciences it was found that contents of courses had a certain value. Researches in experimental psychology proved that we can not conclusively say that ability acquired in one situation is likely to be transferred in toto in another situation.

This gives rise to Thorndike's theory of limited transfer. This assumes that if situations are similar, some transfer of the traits acquired in one situation may take place. Experiments made by the Gestalt psychologists like Kohler, however, shows that the individual does not remember an isolated experience, but the whole field, and since the whole field can not be recalled, there is really no effective transfer possible. Other educators criticise Thorndike's theory of limited transfer as superfluous, for after all, if two situations are identical, what is happening is not transfer, but merely an added practice. It is the practice that offers facility in the solution of difficulty in the second situation. The question is on the significance of developing certain desirable school habits.

Provided a certain thing has been learnt in a wider context, something, be it transfer or repeated practice, remains to be used in another situation. Modern educators, therefore, try to develop the desirable attitudes and offer subjects for instruction and greatest opportunities for enrichment of experience and practice. The habit thus formed in the school environment will be useful in the social environment. In this case the school situation and the social situation become more or less identical. Thus the basic conflicts or problems of life are really brought inside the school-room for the child to solve. No matter whether by providing opportunities for transfer or by giving added practice it would at any rate give him the power to meet the basic conflicts of real life situation. Thus to connect the school with life seems to be the objective of our study of the problem of transfer of training. It is thus really not a transfer of training, but training for transfer that we look forward to.

Teacher as on evaluator

The teacher has multiple roles and functions in different situations in the context of education. He, not only teaches, he has also the function as an evaluator. The purpose of the evaluation is to measure the output of his teaching as well as the outcome of the learning by his pupils. Thus evaluation helps to review the methods of teaching in the class-room and revise in the light of the results of the review.

There are certain tools and techniques of measurement and evaluation, no doubt; yet a resourceful teacher has a scope to develop his own tests of different kinds for the purpose of assessing pupil's behaviour. He may start building up a battery of ad hoc tests for measuring the achievement of the pupils and he may supplement them by diagnostic tests. In short, testing programme should evolve out of the needs. It is only a part of the total evaluation which should be designed for probing into the various areas of the pupil's performance, learning, achievement, attitude and personality. The purpose of testing should be quite clear and the principles of evaluation should be followed in every situation. Recently attempt has been made to integrate testing with teaching as it is believed that teaching and testing should go together. It is observed that the pupils in the class-room differ not only in intelligence but also in interest, attitude and many other personality traits. It is also experienced that the pupil's achievement does not only depend upon intelligence: so many factors can be attributed to the success or failure in pupil's academic life.

Obviously, the teacher has the obligation to know the individual differences precisely for counselling and guidance. In order to know the individual differences, he has to take recourse to testing and observation within the class-room as well as in different school-situations. Sophisticated testing is not always feasible in the limited time available to the teacher. Yet he needs to have an objective assessment of the basic differences in terms of his pupil's potential. It becomes practical to combine the different techniques of assessment including rating and case-studies. I.Q. testing has become fashionable in certain quarters in spite of its limits and limitations. It is a common experience that pupil's work-habit, motivation and persistence contribute no less than intelligence to the pupil's achievement in the classroom. Moreover, statistics indicate that about two-third of the population has around average intelligence. Thus not much is achieved from practical point of view by using the time-consuming intelligence-tests. In stead it is profitable to know the pupil's functional general abilities through his class-room interaction and performance. What is more important is the qualitative analysis instead of the quantitative measurement of the cognitive aspects of the pupil's behaviour. Numerical marking is therefore being replaced by qualitative grading in many progressive countries as it serves a better and perhaps more practical purpose of evaluation.

As testing is but one form of evaluation, there are other methods including rating scales, check list, situational tests and observations. It is a fact that each method has its own limits and limitations and the teacher has the responsibility to make the best use of them. In many cases the subjectivity factor creeps in and undesirable bias of the teacher-evaluator vitiates the purpose of testing. Of course there are measures to increase objectivity of the tests and examination procedure through adequate care and caution. The teacher should be aware of the ways and means which would make evaluation meaningful.

13

GROWTH, DEVELOPMENT AND EDUCATION

Human growth is related to the inherent process of development at various stages in different areas. In spite of the mystery around the process certain consistent patterns are noticeable in the dynamic life of a growing individual. Development involves an orderly progression from lower to higher levels. Rates and forms of development, however, depend upon the environmental stimuli although true developmental sequences are universal. Theory of Cognitive development provides information about how students learn and perceive at different levels. It also offers clue as to how they may be taught most effectively. In fact, development takes place simultaneously at various levels and not in isolated areas. Thus the teacher has to consider the total developmental process including physical, emotional social and cognitive development. Piaget's four major stages mainly viz (i) sensory motor, (ii) pre-operational, (iii) concrete operational, and (iv) formal operational—appear to involve qualitative differences in learning orientations and capacities as well as in cognitive structures. We learn what we do and therefore, learning is abstraction from action. All learning is said to involve both assimilation and accommodation. The children assimilate stimulus features into existing schemes and accommodate the existing schemes into modified or new schemes. Thus Piagetians see people in continuous dynamic interaction with the environment. Assimilation of familiar aspects and accommodation of those to unfamiliar ones continues until a state of equilibrium is reached. The students at the pre-operational stages (early primary grades) learn facts. Creativity is another area belonging to cognitive domain which deserves special mention with reference to human development. It is obvious that the proposed stages of development vary from psychologist to psychologist. For example Freud, Erikson and others have proposed stage-theories of social and personal development while Piaget has stressed the cognitive development for explaining human growth. Similarly Berg's stages of the development of moral judgment refer to the cognitive but not the affective aspects of life.

There is often a confusion around the concepts of 'growth' and 'development'. Development is, no doubt, more comprehensive as a concept as it implies something more than growth. No doubt development occurs during growth but it may also occur when no growth is observable. No matter, whether growth and development are supplementary as concepts for explaining the dynamic process of maturation, education plays a vital role in the area of cognitive development. It facilitates the developmental process by creating suitable stimuli and environment. Environment is very significant as a contributory factor in the area of development. For example, developments in language depend upon the language spoken in the country in which one is born.

Basic to developmental psychology is the concept of stage involving sequence. It is a gradual process, no doubt, but it involves a series of qualitatively distinct stages. Thus, the learning theorists differ from the developmental psychologists in the basic approach to understand life. When applied to education the developmental model places heavy stress on the concepts of maturation and readiness.

It may be worthwhile to make certain observations on the implication of the various theories of learning and motivation. While cognitive theories stress perceptions and thinking, motivational theories attempt to explain the initiation, direction, persistence and intensity of goal-directed behaviour, Behaviourist theory, on the other hand, stresses reinforcement through reward and positive feedback. Teachers may, however, take advantage of all these theories by applying them in class-room situations appropriately, They can also take advantage of intellectual curiosity, achievement, needs and other motivations by using suitable materials, examples and stimulating questions. A basic motivational goal for teachers is to help students, look upon school-tasks as challenging and enjoyable.

Cognitive explanations of behaviour emphasise the role of person's thinking about what is happening to him or his perception of reality. This has been supported by a number of studies which illustrate that cognitive perceptions are real as they influence behaviour.

As mentioned earlier, the concept of need is related to the dynamics of behaviour as Murray defined it as a construct that stands for a force and organises perception.

Few psychologists today corroborate the view that Murray provides a way of looking at differential interest patterns that students bring to the class-room. Although interest is potentially a source of activity or behaviour, it goes without saying that they may differ widely. The teacher can identify and build upon these interests, he can also allow the students to grow from the past history of positive reinforcement. A systematic exposure to environmental stimulations will, no doubt, lead to the development of the dominant interests. The teachers should take note of the wide variety of the student's interests and to integrate them through curricular and co-curricular activities. It's a failure on the part of the teacher to ignore student's interests as a source of motivation and learning. Today, we find student's frustrations finding their expression through anti-social activities. At the root of this frustration of-course we may find the unfulfilled needs including love-needs and other emotional needs, Even the students need for esteem and appreciation has to be respected for the development of a balanced personality. The knowledge of the developmental principles helps the teacher to understand the pupils in a realistic perspective.

In the present context of education we find a dismal picture of the student - life full of confusion and insecurity. They are torn between extremes, between love and hate, courage and cowardice. Education, as such is hardly offering any solution to the crisis at home, in the class-room and community. Thus the consequences of educating children need to be well visualised and strategies built up accordingly. Piaget was one of the psychologists to recognise that human beings are born as active, exploratory and information processing organism. He looks upon people's adoptive activities as more fundamental and important than the external stimuli. His basic unit of cognition, speech and behaviour forms the scheme which he uses rather loosely. The two fundamental mechanisms in the formation and use of all schemes are accommodation and assimilation. In other words, human beings grow as a result of their new learning, adaptation and assimilation. It is important that the differences in rates of acquisition of schemes should be recognised as outcome of the following factors :—

(a) Maturation

(b) Individual experience

(c) Social transmission

(d) Internal Self-direction.

In short, the concepts used by Piaget are useful to a teacher for understanding the processes used by human beings to interact with and adopt to their environment.

14

THEORIES OF CHILD DEVELOPMENT

In summarizing Piaget's theory, we can see that the substance of his findings is very relevant to the educator along with the methods he employs. The method by which he collects data is frequently referred to as "clinical method," which means that the child actively searches for the solution of the problem. The examiner stimulates and challenges the child to reflect on his own answers and to use this discourse as a means to clarify his own thought. Piaget wholeheartedly believes in the child's autonomy and his active participation in his own cognitive growth.

Applying Piaget's findings about children's cognitive growth to teaching could have a revolutionary impact on the planning of the curriculum. The content itself would be influenced or the logical processes by which we think and by which we attempt to solve problems could become a major area of focus in any educational endeavor. Thus there would be a more systematic emphasis on systems of classification, on reversibility, on logical transformations, and on the process of logic in general.

In conclusion, Jean Piaget's theory demonstrates that there are regular patterns in cognitive development which are experienced by everyone. Such an understanding allows us to predict is an individual modes and range of comprehension all along his course of development.

The next theory to be discussed is that of Freud. Freud's theory of development holds that the young child goes through five definite phases in the first five or six years of life and only two more in the remaining fifteen childhood and adolescent years. One of Freud's basic assumptions is that the first five years of childhood are the most formative ones for personality development.

During the oral stage, the child gets pleasurable auto-erotic stimulation from such manipulations of the oral erogenous zone as sucking, drinking, and eating. In the second phase of this oral stage, the oral-sadistic stage, the child exhibits sadistic tendencies through biting during the cutting of teeth. At the end of the second year, the anal stage begins, changing the source of pleasure from the oral to the anal region. He "holds back" and "lets go" to get more pleasure and to exert power over his parents. The oral and anal stages are sometimes called pre-ego periods, since the id impulses are not yet restrained by the ego.

One basic Freudian concept concerns libidinal forces. "Libidinal" energy will have to be defined as the yet unknown force which directs human development. Terms such as "drive, desire, and urge" may be "libidinal energy." This force or energy, which in part is sexual, must be realized as an aspect of the human system.

Freud believed that these forces were attached to various experiences throughout the life of an individual. Therefore it would seem valuable to define these three levels. One is the conscious experience, all those life events which remain within the individual's perceptual and/or cognitive awareness. The second is preconscious experience, which are all those events beyond the individual's immediate recognition but within the realm of his conscious recall. And the third is unconscious experience, which is entirely beyond the individual's perceptive and rational awareness. I have mentioned the above levels of experience because the last two have become the center of most psychoanalytic investigations, and are seen as the most potent determinants of all human motivation.

These libidinal energies from three major analytic processes, are known as the Freudian triad of id, ego, and superego. The id comprises the sum of the "pressure of excessive wishes." This pressure originates in unconscious libidinal energy. The id possesses, further, the unfulfilled libidinal striving of an organism. In other words, the id is all the desires which we must overcome to be human, and not to be mere creatures. The ego is charged with controlling the conscious actions of an individual. It is a combination of all his past experiences which confront him and help him to take actions in the present. The superego is assumed to be made up of personal experiences which have been affected by the higher ideals and attitudes of significant adults and peers in the life of the individual.

The phallic phase—sometimes referred to as "little puberty" begins with interest in manipulation of the sex organs. Infantile masturbation and "impulses for knowledge and investigation" appear in this phase. His newly developed intellectual curiosity draws the child to the problem of sex. The discovery of the ego accompanies the beginning of narcissism. The development of the ego changes the child's total outlook toward the world.

At puberty, the sexual impulses break through to produce the subordination of all sexual component-instincts under the primacy of the genital zone. Whereas pleasure-seeking was the aim of all the infantile forms of sexuality, physiological pubertal changes create another sexual aim, that of reproduction. This phase of psychosexual development is called the genital stage. Pubescent sexuality manifests itself in three different ways : (a) through external stimulation of the erogenous zones: (b) through internal tension and a physiological need to release sexual products, a condition not present in the childhood sexuality; and (c) through psychological "Sexual excitation" which may be influenced by the former two.

Pubescent development not only awakens sexuality, but also enormously increases nervous excitement, anxiety, genital phobia, and personality disturbances "because of the outstanding power of the "lust dynamism". Biological changes bring about behavioural changes, since one's lust collides with one's security. During adolescence, therefore, a person is especially vulnerable to the development of psychopathology.

Increased sexual tension during adolescence revives many of the old incestuous objects of the phallic period. Freud speaks of a second oedipal situation during pubescence. Freud comments that during adolescence a boy's first serious love object is most likely to be a mature woman, and a young girl's an older man-that is, mother and father figures.

But these are not the greatest dangers an adolescent faces in his further development. There exists the danger that friendship ties that are too strong will bind boys and girls to their own sex, with the possibility of inversion of the sex object. Related to the oedipal situation is the adolescent's task of freeing himself from his dependency upon his parents. The boy's libidinal attachment to his mother has to be released and he must also free himself from the dominance of the father. Unsuccessful attempts to resolve either situation will result in neurosis, since they will interfere with the selection of a heterosexual love object. The main task of the adolescent as seen by psychoanalytic theory may be summarized as being the "attainment of genital primacy and the definitive completion of the process of non-incestuous object finding".

It is assumed that the stages of psychosexual development are predominantly biological in nature, since they occur in a predetermined sequence. The biological nature of Freud's theory is further emphasized by the frequent use of the instinct concept. In his earlier theory, the two biological instincts are self-preservation and reproduction. The self-preservation instinct includes such ego motives as hunger, fear, and self-assertion. The reproductive instinct is sexual and in closely related to the physical energy called libido.

In summarizing thus far, Freud assumes that the emotional (libidinal) aspects of life permeate all human functions. Freud is very much concerned with the emotional relationships between persons. Each individual's life—his manner of perceiving, thinking, doing, and feeling—depends largely upon the relative balance of the three major affective processes—the id, the ego, and the superego.

ERIK ERIKSON'S THEORY

Erik Erikson modifies the Freudian theory of psychosexual development in the light of findings by cultural anthropology. The core concept in his theory of ego development is the acquiring of ego identity. This a accomplished in different ways from culture to culture. However, there is one common element which is present in all cultures, namely the idea that the child must receive consistent, meaningful recognition of his achievements and accomplishments. In each of the eight developmental steps that Erikson describes a conflict with two possible outcomes arises. If the conflict is worked out in a satisfactory manner, the positive quality is built into the ego and further healthy development can take place. But if the conflict is resolved unsatisfactorily, the developing ego is damaged.

Here is a list of the eight basic stages in chronological order-comparing them to corresponding Freudian stages:—

(1)	Trust vs. mistrust	Oral sensory
(2)	Autonomy vs. shame and doubt	Muscular anal

(3)	Initiative vs. guilt	Locomotor genital
(4)	Industry vs. inferiority	Latency ,
(5)	Identity vs. role diffusion	Puberty and adolescence
(6)	Intimacy vs. isolation	Young adulthood
(7)	Generativity vs. stagnation	Adulthood
(8)	Ego integrity vs. disgust, despair	Maturity

Pubescence, according to Erikson is characterized by rapidity of body growth, genital maturity, and sexual awareness. Youth is confronted with a "physiological revolution" within himself that threatens his body image and his ego identity. He becomes preoccupied with what he "appears to be in the eyes of others" as compared with what he feels he is. Adolescence is the period during which a dominant positive ego identity is to be established. Erikson maintains that the study of identity has become as important as the study of sexuality was in Freud's time. Particularly as for the adolescent, identity (which is the establishment of sameness with one's previous experiences and a conscious attempt to make the future a part of one's personal life plan) becomes subordinated to sexuality. If ego identity is not satisfactorily established at this stage, there is the danger that role diffusion will endanger further ego development. Where this is based on a strong previous doubt as to one's sexual identity, delinquent and outright psychotic incidents are not uncommon.

Vocational identity is still a great concern for many adolescents. During the initial attempts to establish ego identity some role diffusion exists. Adolescents at this time frequently over-identify with movies heroes, group leaders, athletic champions, etc. At this point, youth rarely identifies with his parents. On the contrary, he rebels against their dominance, their value system, and their intrusion into his private life, since he has to separate his identity from that of his parents. However, there is a desperate need for social belonging. The peer group and gang help the individual in finding his own identity in a social context. Particularly during the time when the body image changes radically, when genital maturity stimulates imagination, and when intimacy with the opposite sex appears as a possibility, the adolescent relies on his peers for comfort by stereotyping himself, his ideals, and his adversaries.

Falling in love, which is a common and frequent occurrence at this age, is not of a sexual nature to the same degree as it will be at later ages. The "serious" love affairs through which the adolescent passes contribute to the development of the ego as one identification succeeds another, and the adolescent is aided in defining and revising his own definition of his ego. Ego identity to be established before marriage should be considered. A person must really know who he is and whom he wants, to become before he can decide who is a suitable mate for him. "Crushes," which occur frequently at the high school and college level, serve a genuine psychological purpose. This is why many would rather converse, and settle matters of mutual identification.

Maturity begins when identity has been established and an integrated, independent individual has emerged. He can now stand on his own feet, without emotional crutches from others.

Ego identity involves total integration of vocational ambitions and aspirations, along with all those qualities acquired through earlier identification, imitation of parents, falling in love, admiration of heroes, etc. Only the achievement of all these aspects of ego identity will permit intimacy of sexual love and deep friendship.

Erikson's contribution of psychological thought is in his systematic reorganization of psychoanalytic theory in the light of anthropological findings. He has gone beyond the preoccupation of orthodox psychoanalysis. He has brought about a shift in emphasis to the social conditions and organizations in which the ego must be rooted for normal development.

Erikson's stages which are similar have been influenced by those of Freud. For example, feeding, and oral function, results in social trust when it is appropriately gratified. Autonomy should be established during the anal period. For the first time, the child will experience the autonomy of free choice in the power of "holding on and letting go when he wishes." Initiative is related to the phallic stage in the boy, which expresses itself in exuberance, a feeling of power, aggressive manipulation, and pleasure in attack. In girls, aggressive initiative may be present in the form of "catching"; it may be modified to making herself more attractive. Industry should develop during the latency period. Unable to marry his mother, the boy now must learn to become a potential provider and to gain recognition so that he may later leave his family and start his own. He must establish ego identity during puberty to incorporate genital maturity into his body image. In this way he establishes a sense of ego integrity, which is essential if he is to enter a genuine love relationship in which he abandons himself. We may conclude, therefore, that the stage concept, in general, is a vital and integral part of all psychoanalytic theories.

In conclusion, Erikson's modified form of psychoanalytic theory offers more helpful advice to the teacher. According tò Erikson, it is not frustration per se that results in neurosis, but frustration that is not meaningful. Therefore, parents and teachers should only introduce culturally meaningful forms of frustration. Erikson assumes that, as part of the process of growing up, children must learn to encounter limits and restrictions which may be frustrating. But they will not produce neurosis so long as they are meaningful. Meaningful ways of frustrating children will challenge them, direct their activities, and bring about learning.

According to Freud, the first stage is the oral level (sucking and swallowing). The over indulged child at the first oral level is characterized as carefree, generous, optimistic, and unwilling to assume responsibilities. The child who is frustrated in his oral needs is said to become pessimistic, demanding of help from others, and dependent. The second oral stage is the oral sadistic (biting, devouring) level. Lack of satisfaction at this level results in an adult characterized by ambivalent attitudes toward others. Friendliness alternates with hostility, aggression with submissiveness, love with hate.

The anal stage follows the oral period. Here the libido becomes concentrated upon the process of the expulsion of feces and the clashes with the parent's needs to train the child. The child who fixated at the anal level of development is dominated by retaining characteristics as an adult. Frustration at this level results either in "regression" back to the oral stage or in personal characteristics of worries about fine details, cleanliness, parsimony, obstinacy, or, in extremity, sadism, or masochism.

The anal period is replaced by the phallic stage (touching, exploring, fantasizing about the genitalia) and the development of the Oedipus complexie, love for the parent of the opposite sex. In normal children the Oedipus complex is resolved as the child abandons the parent as a love object and identifies with the parent of the same sex. It is through this process that the superego (conscience) is formed and strengthened.

The latency period of middle childhood is a time of libidinal quiescence, during which repression and other psychological "defense mechanisms" appear, and social feelings develop. Puberty brings on the late genital period, a revival of the Oedipus conflict, the development of adult modes of libidinal satisfaction, the pre-dominance of homosexual choice, and finally the normal heterosexual choice of the love object.

The cognitive growth process is very complicated. Every child has some experiences and the environment has impact on us and therefore we attend to it. Yet, some children are curious and seek further information while others are withdrawn. Children do differ in respect of responsiveness and receptivity. Through interaction children absorb, assimilate, classify, organize and reinforce.

Educational Application of Development Principles

The objectives of teaching and learning are obviously related to the stages of development of the pupils and their capacity or potential. It is therefore, likely that the teacher has to be aware of various types of development viz.

(a) Physical Development,
(b) Cognitive Development,
(c) Language Development,
(d) Social Development, and
(e) Emotional and personality Development.

It is important that the child grows in all directions simultaneously as a human being. As his body grows, his mental function also starts at various levels. The most fundamental implication of development at psychology for education is that Educational experiences must be matched with cognitive and other developments of the learners. This can be done in a general way because most individuals of the same age range will be roughly at the same developmental level. Education involves optimizing instruction to meet the unique needs of each student. However, it is essential to recognise that cognitive development takes place rather slowly. Pupils acquire knowledge and skill as they grow.

According to Piaget, development in inherent, dynamic and continuous. The teacher should have definite ideas of the characteristic at each stage of child development. Otherwise his understanding of the pupils will remain incomplete. The developmental considerations thus help a teacher in meeting the individual needs of each child.

15

GROUP BEHAVIOUR

Men live in groups and are guided at times by group life and its norms. Their individual reaction is modified and their behaviour is adjusted and controlled by the social environment.

No doubt, the basic instincts and needs prompt our activities for their satisfaction. Yet they undergo certain modifications under group pressure. This is because man is basically a social creature. Group life generates new needs and expectations. Values and attitudes thus shape group behaviour. Satisfaction plays a prominent part in group behaviour. Individuals while interacting with one another tend to gain from their individual course of action. A group mindedness prevails when individuals sacrifice their strong individuality and come to a compromise for better adjustment. Individuals need company and co-operation for effective functioning. Man can not live alone in isolation. He is particularly a social animal. It is impossible for man to live in an environment cut off from other members of the community. His innate urge to co-operate and coordinate is strong.

Group life offers the child a social environment. The individual child needs love, encouragement and sense of security within the family and group. Without the group life the child hardly grows. Group interaction helps the child to grow socially and emotionally. Thus when a child comes to school he learns together and shares his experience.

He gets the opportunity to express his feeling of self-assertion, communion and combat and grows up emotionally, socially and physically. As mentioned earlier, the child grows through experience. He needs sympathy and suggestion for self expansion. At time a child feels dependent and looks forward to suggestions and sympathy from his groups. Sympathy provides sense of security and builds up the ego strength of the child.

At times a child is confused or defused and badly needs suggestion. The role of parents, teachers and even of friends is very significant.

Sympathy is the fellow feeling or feeling with others. This involves emotions when shared among members within a group. Emotion is aroused in case there is any accident or a sudden situation demanding common participation.

It facilitates social solidarity and brings harmony of actions even around an occasion or event.

Sympathy also plays a significant role in animal behaviour. It prompts them to share and profit from each others experience and knowledge of a group life. Sympathy may be expressed both in active and passive forms.

In a class room situation the teachers can take advantage of their interaction by arousing emotions for the right and good cause among the pupils. He can inspire them toward noble causes and creative activities.

Like sympathy, imitation is found to influence group behaviour, to love others instinctively as this tendency is ingrained in nature since childhood. A child learns to speak gradually. He copies from nearest adults other's behaviours even unconsciously. Imitation is very common when the relationship between the members is close and cordial. We imitate what we admire in others.

The children learn most by imitating their parents and teachers. Most of the habits and modes of behaviour are copied by children through imitation. Imitation is great social bond, a means of uniting a large number of individuals into one group.

Group behaviour is dominant when there is cohesion and communality. Group behaviour is something more than a collective behaviour.

Motivation and interest can be generated by applying group dynamics. Not only in the field of education, group dynamics are applied at present even in the field of industry for better production.

Cooperation, competition and conflict are the various modes of group behaviour which can be employed for producing the behaviour as end result.

In the present society we find competition and conflict more than cooperation. There is a struggle for survival of the fittest. It is the law of the present society. We can hardly ignore this stark reality. Yet there are certain occasions and causes which demand cooperation, and co-ordination for our greater interest. Any national enterprise demands co-operation in spite of conflicts and competitions within group.

Group Behaviour and Education

With the growing size of the class room and increasing load of curriculum there is hardly any time to pay individual attention in the class room. It is also not feasible to treat pupils individually. The present situation thus demands application of group dynamics, where a class is divided into groups for participation in assigned educational activities. This interactional approach very often proves economic and effective as well.

In group approach an individual finds it possible to contribute his best to the group performance and develops a sense of identity with the group. The spirit of social awareness is thus stimulated through this group activity.

16

CONFLICT—THE ROLE OF THE UNCONSCIOUS

Mind refers to the human thought, feelings emotions and desires, memories and motives. The contents of our mind may be analysed or observed by instrospection while some of our behaviours can not be explained by analysing our conscious mind. The conscious process can not always explain our certain behaviours.

There are certain disconnected thoughts and actions which have no connection with conscious process. There are hidden dimensions of our cognitive behaviour which we call unconsciousness.

In fact, conscious life consists of a small part of our mental life.

Group behaviour which is often the outcome of social pressure is guided mostly by the social desirability.

There are certain social instincts which are stimulated by the presence of other human beings. For example, there are instincts of self preservation, self assertion, gregariousness which are quite in keeping with the social awareness and sense of dignity.

Some writers like Hobbes considers rivalry as an innate disposition and a spirit of competition behind conflict.

Others consider 'herd' instinct playing significant role behind co-operation and conflict at times. In short, so many innate dispositions work behind the group behaviour.

As mentioned earlier, some general tendencies play their part in shaping our group behaviour. Not all of them can be traced at the conscious level. Most of our conflict have their root at the subconscious and unconscious levels. Imitation, sympathy and suggestions are the tendencies of the individual to take from other's modes of behaviour.

General tendencies are not the same as specific instincts which are aroused in specific situations. Conflict arises when our basic needs or desires are obstructed. This creates conflict or confusion.

When we are not able to decide and act when more than one idea or impulse tries to lead us to opposite courses of action, we face conflict. Conflict and hesitation are painful, no doubt. The mind becomes divided and it fails to meet any difficult situation with confidence or competence. Struggles go on and the state of conflict at the unconscious level become quite uncomfortable. At times one has to face situation leading to conflict of values and brings a scope of repression of socially unacceptable desires.

Some of the repressed wishes seek expression through dreams. Our unfulfilled desires sometime find their outlet through dreams. Psychoanalysts often use dream for explaining human behaviour at the unconscious or subconscious levels.

Repression is often taken recourse to by children to adjust to complex environment. It is also frequent in adult life.

It is hardly accessible to reasoning as it lies at the unconscious level. It is often claimed that repression is at the root of many mental disorders. They express themselves in dreams when some of the wished get an opportunity for free expression when self control and social checks are at the lowest.

Freud, Jung and others support interpretation of dreams for explaining our unfulfilled desires. In school situation, we find conflicts at various levels. There is conflict among children, among teachers, among students, teachers and parents. They are around various issues and roles. At present with the emergence of democracy in our education and schools we try to resolve the conflicts after proper diagnosis. When we have adopted the principle of democracy we have to accept the method of government of the people, for the people, and by the people. This approach reduces the scope for conflict for obvious reasons.

Besides co-operation, sympathy and suggestion very often play important roles for resolving the conflict.

Suggestion is an effective means of avoiding conflict and confrontation. A policy of give and take helps to come to understanding before the conflict states. It is often seen that suggestion comes from above for acceptance at the lower level. But it is not always so.

It goes without saving that repression at times is a necessity for the development of a complex. The formation of complex helps conflict resolution as complex is an idea or a group of ideas strongly mixed with emotion that is repressed. The moral standard or customs do not permit the display of many crude complexes which acknowledges failure to cope with the demands of a challenging situation of life. Complexes are, therefore not always desirable as they may adversely effect personality. There are certain hobbies and obsessions which may become complexes. Yet they may contribute to socialization and community life. Exchanging visits and small gifts to sick friends are helpful to develop a social outlook.

Repression is quite common both in the life of children and adults. There are wishes which are not allowed to be expressed in social life and they find their place in the unconscious. They also seek their outlet in the dreams. There are certain symptoms of mental conflict like scratching the head, movement of legs during conversation, struggling shoulders, frequent winking and stammering. Frequent ships and omissions may be caused by conflicts as well.

Lying among school children may be due to repression.

Abnormal forgetting usually takes place as we tend to forget the unpleasant experiences and things.

The teacher and parents should realize the evil effect of repression on child mind. The child's personality may be thwarted and turned into neurotic as a result of too much pressure.

Mental conflicts and mental hygiene

Mental health is an important asset in every life. Life calls for adjustment to any change in environment, physical and social. It is through adjustment one maintains a balance between his needs and circumstances. A person can hardly find satisfaction unless he can make effective adjustment.

BIBLIOGRAPHY

ADMAS JEMES T., A Study of Adult Education and Frontier of American Cen.

ALEXANDER SAMUEL, Space Time and Deity, MacMillan 1920.

ALLPORT G. W., Personality Harper, N.V. 1947.

BURN MICHAEL, Scientific and Education, H. Hamilton 1956.

BRUBACHER JOHNS, Modern Philosophies of Education.

CAMPBELL C. A., Selfhood and Godhood, Allen and Unwin 1957.

COOK CALDWELL,Playway in Education, Hutchinson 1961.

CURTIS S. J., An Introduction to the Philosophy of Education.

EWING A. C., Second Thoughts on Moral Philosophy Routledge.

FOSTER MICHAEL, In Mystery and Philosophy S.C.M. Press, London 1957.

FLEW AG. N. (ED.), Essays in Conceptual Analysis, MacMillan 1956

HUME, A Treatise of Human Nature Part—4.

HENRY NELSON, Education in Rural Communities, Chicago Univ. Press.

KANT IMMANUEL, Fundamental Principles of the Metaphysics and Ethics, Longmans 1911.

LINTO RALPH, The Cultural Background of Personality, Applenton Century Co.

LANDIS PAUL H., Man In Environment, N.Y.

MACMURRAY JOHN, The Form of the Personal—The Self as an agent, Faber London 1957.

MILTON G., Genius and Creativity, Harper N.Y 1965.

PERCY NUNN, Education--Its data and First Principles.

PEEPER JOSEPH, Leisure of Bans of Culture, Faber.

PROGRAMMING FOR WORLD AFFAIRS, Adult Leadership (July-August 1933).

ODHUM HOWARD W., Understanding Society, MacMillan Co. N.Y. 1947.

REID A.L., Ways of Knowledge and Experience, Allen and Unwin.

PERSCOTT DANIEL, Emotion and the executive Process, American Council of Education, Washington D.C.

SERGENT S. and SMITH, Culture and Personality.

SMITH B. O. et al., Foundations of Curriculum Improvement World Book Co. 1953.

WELLING M. H. et al, School and our Democratic Society, Harper and Brother N. Y.

SOCIOLOGICAL FOUNDATION

CHAPLIN F.S., Cultural Change.

COOK L. A., A Sociological Approach to Education Book Co. 1950.

DAVIS ALLISON, Social Class Influences upon learning, Harvard University Press 1945.

DAVIS KINGSLEY, Human Society, MacMillan Co. 1949.

FOSTER R. G., Marriage and Family Relations, MacMillan Co., N.Y. 1930

HENRY NELSON B., Education in Rural Communities — Chicago University Press 1982

H. FRANCIS I, Man and Society, Appleton Century N.Y.

JONES MARSHALL E., Basic Sociological Principles.

LINTON RALPH, The Cultural Background of Personality Appleton Century Co.,

MEAD MARGARET, Growth and Culture Pitman's Sons, N.Y.

MURRAY RAYMOND W., Sociology for a Democratic Society, Appleton Century N.Y. 1950.

SERGENT. S. S. and SMITH M., Culture and Personality.

SILVERMAN LEO, Analysis of Society, William Hodge and Co., London 1951.

PSYCHOLOGICAL FOUNDATION

ANDERSON JOHN E., The Psychology of Development and Personal Adjustment, Henny Holt & Co. N.Y. 1951.

DAVIS ALLISON, Social Class Influences upon learning. Harvard University Press.

GUILFORD J.P. Editor, Fields of Psychology Basic and applical, D:Vasc Nostrand N.Y.

MUNN NORMAN L., Psychology The Fundamentals of Human Adjustment, Houghton Heffin Co. Boston 1943.

MURPHY GARDNER, Psychology An Introduction to Psychology, Harper and Brothers N.Y. 1951

MUNRUE WALTER S., Teaching Learning-Theory and Teacher Education, University of Illinois Press 1952.

ROSE, Groundwork of Educational Psychology (Har etc.)

SKINNER B.F., Educational Psychology Prentice Hall.

STAGNER ROSS, Psychology of Personality, Mc Graw Hill N.Y. 1948

THORNDIKE, Educational Psychology.

VERNON P. E., The Structure of Human Abilities

VERNON P.E., Personality Tests and Assessments, Methum & Co. Ltd. 1953

VULKART EDMAND H., Social Behaviour and Personality, Social Science Research Council.

WOODWORTH R., Psychology, Methum.

YOUNG, Motivation of Behaviour Waley.

